Love For Lillian

Written by: *Sarah Wilson*
Edited by: *Judi Ludwig*
Cover created by: *Marissa Campeau* (Graphic Designer)

ISBN: 9781720157977
Imprint: Independently published

Dedicated to:

Lillian Wilson. *Beautiful baby, you have fought bigger battles during your first sixteen months of life than most people fight in their entire lives. Not only do I admire your resilience in the face of adversity, but I also appreciate your strength and bravery. You are the most courageous little girl in the world. You continue to bounce back against all odds. Keep fighting, sweet baby girl. Always remember that your beauty marks display your breathtaking story of survival to the world. I love you and could not be prouder to be your mommy.*

Preslee Wilson. *My caring and compassionate daughter, you have shown a stronger love for your sister than any love I have ever seen between siblings. Your life has changed drastically, yet you have handled every situation that arises without complaint, just like a true champ. You are especially sweet to your sissy, always wanting to make her boo-boos go away. Lillian is incredibly fortunate that God has chosen you to be her sister, and I am thankful and blessed to have you for my daughter. I love you and am proud of you, princess.*

Lillian's heart surgeon (Dr. H), cardiologist (Dr. G), and all of the phenomenal nurses and doctors we have met along the way. *We can never thank you enough for believing in Lillian and saving her life multiple times. If not for you, we wouldn't have our sweet baby girl. You have become like a second family to us, and our lives are a gazillion times better with you in them. We love you, and we love your staff. We'll see you next time and not a day sooner!*

In Memory of
Logan Vanderkleed (October 9, 2014-August 24, 2017)

I was so sad to learn of Logan's passing. He did not deserve to die when he was only two. It was a freak accident for which any parents would beat themselves up. I thank the Vanderkleed family for allowing Logan to give my Lillian the gift of life. His aortic valve and other heart tissue will always be well taken care of in Lillian's heart. Logan will forever be a part of her, which makes her heart even more special. If I could change all of this and give Logan back to his loving family, I would do it in a heartbeat.

*Several names have been changed to protect the identity of the person or institution mentioned, including the hospital at which Lillian was treated, along with the cardiovascular heart surgeon and pediatric cardiologist. I think too highly of them to assign them a "fake" name, so I will refer to them as Dr. H (heart surgeon), Dr. G (cardiologist), and "the hospital."

*Numerous medical terms are used throughout the book because they have become everyday household words for us and other parents who are raising a baby who has been diagnosed with a congenital heart defect. I have tried to define these terms in language any reader can understand. They are now woven into our vocabulary and our life, and I couldn't fully tell Lillian's story without them.

Table of Contents

Chapter 1
The 26-Week Ultrasound

Lillian's story begins in the waiting room at my ob-gyn clinic, where my husband, Jeramy, and I are waiting anxiously for the technician to call my name. Our two-year-old daughter, Preslee, has tagged along and is happily browsing through the collection of children's books. I'm 26 weeks pregnant, and we're here to get an ultrasound of our baby. We had a genetic screening test performed prior to this appointment and were happy to learn that all of the tests revealed our pregnancy and baby were "low risk." To us this means we are going to have a "healthy" baby ... or so we think.

Initially, we had wanted to know the baby's gender but later made the decision to wait. As we sit here now, Jeramy and I are discussing how ecstatic we are to *not* find out the baby's gender and how exciting it is to be so far along in the pregnancy. Many friends and relatives would say to us, "How can you possibly wait to find out the baby's gender? There is no way we could wait that long. Surely you want to know what you're having." It seemed as though everyone wanted to know the baby's gender except us. On one hand, we *did* want to know, so we could prepare for his or her arrival; on the other hand, because we knew this baby would be our last, we were thankful to simply have a baby, male or female, growing inside me again. We would always smile and reply, "We don't care what we are having as long as it's healthy." Those words slipped out of our mouths easily and frequently without much thought because we continually had to say them to individuals who inquired about our baby's gender.

We were naive to think that because the genetic screening showed the baby to be low risk, that statistic alone meant we were having a healthy baby. We also didn't understand at that time how special a child is who has a chronic illness. Soon we would realize, however, that having a baby, healthy or not, would be the biggest blessing in our lives. All that mattered to us was the fact that we were having a baby—a living, breathing little person!

We keep glancing at the clock in the waiting room because we know that, following this appointment, we must quickly head home. Jeramy's mom and stepdad are en route from Kentucky to meet us at our house in DeSoto, Missouri, to spend the weekend. I always treasure the time we get to spend with them during these visits because we don't get to see them as often as we would like. I especially love that they choose to stay at our house rather than a hotel. We have planned a few activities for their visit because Jeramy's birthday is coming up and we want to celebrate it with his family. One of the highlights will be dinner with his parents, brother, and nephews. Perhaps best of all, we are overjoyed that we will be able to show his family more ultrasound pictures of our baby. Without a doubt, it is going to be a memorable weekend.

While we continue to wait for my name to be called, I join Preslee at a small wooden table in the corner of the waiting room, where we begin to read books to each other. Another little girl about the same age as Preslee is also here. My heart is filled with joy as I watch my daughter interact with this child. Preslee pulls out books from the small bookshelf and hands them one by one to the other child. If she will not accept a book, Preslee carefully places it on the table next to her. I am thinking about what a loving and caring big sister Preslee will make when, without warning, the little girl tries to grab a book out of Preslee's hand. I am shocked to see my normally thoughtful and considerate daughter yell at the girl and try to smack her away. I am quickly yanked back to reality, however, by the realization that my darling daughter doesn't quite grasp the concept of sharing just yet.

Despite Preslee's little tantrum, we are glad we have brought her with us to this appointment. We can't wait to see the look on her face when she sees her new baby brother or sister for the first time on the computer screen. We definitely want her to play a big part in this journey so that she will be prepared for the changes that will take place when the baby arrives and will be excited by her upcoming role as a big sister.

"Sarah," the nursing assistant calls my name. Thank goodness, because the book fiasco is about to get out of hand very quickly, and my daughter is sure to display her full-blown terrible twos in a matter of seconds. She is like a ticking time bomb! I hurry to put the books back on the shelf, allowing Preslee to take one into the examining room with her in hopes that I can prevent the complete meltdown that is about to happen. Luckily for me, my ingenuity works.

"How are you today?" the nursing assistant greets me. "We're going to perform your exam first because our ultrasound technician is out of the office today, and we are waiting for another to come in. Please go ahead and step on the scale for me. Will you be able to provide a urine sample today?"

All I can think about now is how I hope the substitute technician will arrive in time to perform my ultrasound. I was so thrilled to see my baby via ultrasound at previous appointments, so I want Jeramy and Preslee to be present for this one. At my 20-week ultrasound, the baby did not cooperate. Its legs were crossed, and the position in which he or she was lying was not conducive for the technician to get a good profile of the body and all views of the heart. I am very happy to be seeing our baby again and am hopeful that the ultrasound will show everything we need to see this time. I am not surprised or nervous to learn that all of the pictures cannot be taken, because this is what happened at my 20-week ultrasound when I was pregnant with Preslee. The technician couldn't get a good profile of the body or views of the heart.

We walk into the examining room, and I answer a few routine questions: "Yes, I am feeling great. No, I do not have any concerns. No new medicines and no morning sickness." I lie back on the table so that the doctor can listen to the baby's heartbeat on the Doppler. "Everything sounds good," she says. "The baby has an awesome heartbeat of 134 beats per minute [bpm]. The other good news is that the ultrasound technician is here. We'll go ahead and get the few pictures we couldn't get at your 20-week ultrasound. After that you are free to leave, and I'll see you at your next appointment." We head straight into the next room. I am excited to be able to see the baby again. Thankfully, Preslee is still absorbed in her book. The appointment seems to be going quickly, which is always a blessing when our toddler comes with us.

"Lie down on the table and lift your shirt over your belly, please," the ultrasound technician says. I make sure to tell her that we do not know or want to know the gender of our baby. She places the warm gel all over my stomach, and there on the screen appears my baby, wiggling all around. I am so happy that I can hardly hold back my tears. We are all laughing because our baby is lying the same way in which I am lying. We both have our left arm positioned under our head and our legs are crossed. We look away when the technician moves the scanner toward the lower half of our baby's body, not wanting to see its gender. She starts asking us questions while continuing to perform the ultrasound. "Was your daughter small?"

"Yes," I respond. "She was six pounds, seven ounces at birth. Why do you ask? Is this baby small too?"

She replies with a simple "Yes."

I don't give much thought to her questions at this time, although I do notice that she is very quiet as she performs our ultrasound. I think her behavior is a bit odd but speculate that she is quiet because she doesn't know us well and doesn't want to slip up and inadvertently tell us the gender of our baby. She finishes the ultrasound and prints some pictures of our baby for us to keep. Preslee is starting to get bored, and I intuitively sense the beginnings of a tantrum. I know she is about to explode, so Jeramy and I quickly do whatever we can to entertain her.

"I am going to ask you to wait in this room over here," the technician says, as she points to a room that I've been in before. "I will check with your doctor to make sure you guys are good to go."

Jeramy informs her that our doctor has already given permission for us to leave after the ultrasound, but she insists that we wait in the room. She states that she normally does not perform the ultrasounds and wants to make sure the doctor doesn't need anything else from us. Not wanting to get her in trouble, we follow her instructions and stay in the room.

Preslee is full of energy by this point. She starts dancing around and acting silly. Laughter begins to fill the small room. I start to tell Preslee the story of how I had sat in this room when I was 39 weeks pregnant with her. She wasn't moving in my stomach as much as the doctor thought she should, so I was hooked me up to a monitor to complete a stress test. The sweet memories of my being pregnant with her start to flood my mind ... until I remember that this is the *comfort room*. This is the room in which I try to relax and remain stress-free. I start to get a bad feeling in my stomach. It's as though I know something is wrong, but I'm not sure exactly what it is that's wrong. Jeramy is becoming impatient and decides that we should just leave, because our doctor has already given us permission to do so. But a part of me wants to stay just to make sure everything is fine with our baby. I look at Jeramy and say, "It's been ten minutes. I sure hope nothing is wrong with our baby's heart."

"No, I'm sure the baby is fine," he replies. "Your doctor is probably just busy." The words are barely out of his mouth when my doctor finally enters the room. As she pulls over a chair and sits down, tears fill my eyes. I know something isn't right, but nothing could have prepared me to hear the words that are about to come out of her mouth. The unspoken rule is that no doctor comes into a room and immediately sits down unless she is about to tell her patient something no one wants to hear. Sadly, my doctor is no exception to this rule

Chapter 2
Where It All Started

To build our family Jeramy and I had to undergo in vitro fertilization (IVF), a medical procedure in which an egg and sperm are fertilized outside of the body and then implanted in a woman. We were unable to have children on our own because Jeramy has cystic fibrosis, (CF), a genetic lung disease that causes severe damage to the lungs, digestive system, and other organs. To date there is no cure. We consulted with fertility specialists for advice on getting pregnant, and they determined that IVF was the best solution. Although we were both very young when we married, we knew that we wanted babies. We also realized that this process could take a very long time, so we did not want to wait too long to begin the procedure. The cost of IVF was just under $20,000, which was a lot of money to us, but we wanted a baby so badly that we would pay whatever it cost. We saved every penny we could, including our tax refund, and put every spare dollar in our baby fund. We also refinanced our car to avoid having to obtain a personal loan.

All of our scrimping and saving paid huge dividends when we were blessed with three embryos on the very first try. We decided to implant one and save the other two. I considered three to be the perfect number because I have always wanted three children. On September 24, 2014, our first fresh embryo transfer took place. I was incredibly nervous, but I listened intently to everything I was told to do. Jeramy accompanied me in the room, and together we watched the doctors implant the embryo. It was such a cool but nerve-wracking time. We waited anxiously for the next two weeks to pass, which seemed like the longest time I have ever had to wait for something. I then had my first beta test, which is a blood test that determines whether or not a woman is pregnant based on hCG (female hormone) levels. The test came back positive for the presence of hCG. Two days later we had our second beta, and hCG levels had tripled! This meant that we were pregnant! We were finally going to be parents. It felt very surreal.

During this process, I was working as a first-year teacher in a very challenging school district. Not only was I trying to learn how to be a good teacher in what I would call a toxic environment, but I also was pregnant with my first baby and trying to avoid stressful situations. This was so hard. There were days when I would drive home and cry the entire way. I didn't understand the environment in which I was working because it was so far removed from the one in which I had been raised. I had to deal with students who were downright cruel. Some would get right in my face and cuss me out. Others would come into my class wearing handcuffs that had been placed on them by security because they had gotten in trouble on the bus. Students who would get into fights in the hallway were sent right back to class because the principals didn't have time to deal with them. I received no support from the administration. For example, when a student shoved me, the principal didn't even reprimand him for his outrageous, and possibly criminal, behavior. Another student cut the cord on my phone so that I couldn't call his mom. The school pinned this on me, classifying the situation as poor classroom management on my part. Working for this district was a nightmare. I was always stressed, and I even contemplated giving up my dream of teaching. I was confident that I possessed the knowledge, skills, and compassion to be an amazing teacher, but I could not teach in this environment under these conditions.

I wanted to get out of there but couldn't. The stress was taking its toll on me, and I knew it couldn't be good for the baby either, but I was stuck. I had no other option. When the district lost its accreditation, the state became involved. It began taking away the teaching licenses of teachers who broke their contracts by quitting. I decided I would not return to work there again. I don't know many teachers who did stay. I now needed to find a new job, another thing that would cause the stress meter to rise.every day I worried that something would be wrong with my baby, but my fears were all for naught.

We met our miracle baby, Preslee, on her due date: June 12, 2015. She was born a healthy 6 pounds, 7 ounces. The moment I laid eyes on her my life forever changed! I now had a purpose in life, which was to be a mother. I was determined to be the best mother I possibly could be and to give my daughter everything she needed and more. I was going to teach her to tie her shoes, to count, to recite the alphabet, and to recognize colors and shapes. I would teach her to be responsible, independent, compassionate, and empathetic so that she would grow up to be a successful member of society. This is what I have always dreamed about, having a little girl who I could dress up in pretty clothes and style her hair in different fashions.

Being a mommy and watching Preslee grow and learn new things is the most rewarding part of my life. I am proud of the little toddler we have raised. When I look at the loving person she has become, I am reassured that Jeramy and I are doing well in life and are raising her the way a child should be raised.

We were now ready to give Preslee a little brother or sister, so we decided to attempt another pregnancy in July 2016. We transferred one frozen embryo in late July, and in early August I had my first beta test. It was positive! Jeramy and I were ecstatic. I was filled with happiness, and nothing was going to break me down. Everything was going as planned. I landed my dream job as a first grade teacher in a better school district. I was happily married, had a beautiful daughter, was meeting new people, and was now pregnant with my second baby. What could go wrong? Well, in my naive mind I thought nothing, because everything had gone so smoothly with my first pregnancy.

Three days later I had my second beta test and patiently waited for the results. When the lab didn't call within a couple of hours to give me the results, as they normally did, I got a gut-wrenching feeling that something just wasn't right.By now it was already mid-afternoon, and I still had not heard anything after waiting for hours. Jeramy kept trying to reassure me that everything was fine, saying that the lab personnel are probably just busy, but I had a bad feeling I just couldn't shake. On my way home from work, I received the phone call that I had been waiting for all day.

"Hello, is this Sarah? Hi, this is Molly. I am calling to let you know that your beta results came back and the levels have dropped down to five. We call this a chemical pregnancy. I am sorry, but you are no longer pregnant. I know this must be hard …"

Everything else she said after that was a blur. My heart was pounding, and tears covered my face. I sobbed and wept in pity for myself and my unborn baby. I pulled into a gas station parking lot and called Jeramy to give him the news. He tried to comfort me, but in that moment nothing he could say would ever take away the emptiness I felt inside. I could feel anger and sadness building up inside me. How could this happen to me? Our first pregnancy was perfect. I had worked in the most stressful job ever, and yet Preslee came out fine. This wasn't supposed to happen to me. I have been told that my body is naturally made for having babies, so never in my wildest dreams did I ever think or fear that I would suffer a miscarriage. I had heard of a "rainbow" baby (a baby who is born after a miscarriage, stillborn, or neonatal death) and had great compassion for their mothers, but in my wildest nightmares, I never dreamed I would be the mother of one. I pulled myself together and drove home. When I arrived, I cried in my husband's arms and then hugged my daughter a little tighter that night. Then, through sobs and tears, I said a prayer, asking God to take care of my precious rainbow baby.

I couldn't help but blame myself. No one could explain to me why this had happened, so I assumed it had to be my fault. When I was pregnant with Preslee, I did everything I was told to do. I was always careful to not overexert myself. With this baby, only a week prior to the beta test, Jeramy and I had decided to go on a small hike with my sister, brother-in-law, their baby, and Preslee. It was such a hot day. I remember getting small cramps in my stomach and praying they were simply growing pains. However, I was only walking; it wasn't like I was running a marathon. I'm a very tiny person, and all of the IVF medicines always caused me to swell up. I knew without a doubt that I was pregnant with Preslee. I could see it in my body's new shape. I was not given any restrictions and thought going for a walk wouldn't hurt this baby but that it would be beneficial to both of us. Whether it was or it wasn't, I will always question whether this short hike was the reason I miscarried my baby.

We had a consultation with our IVF specialist a couple of weeks after my miscarriage and decided to try one last time for another baby. We desperately wanted another child, and we had one frozen embryo left. We had already spent what little money we had saved on the pregnancy that ended in miscarriage, so our only option was to refinance Jeramy's motorcycle to pay for the last embryo to be implanted in me. We kept it a secret and didn't let anyone know we were going through the process again. On September 20, 2016, we went to the clinic, knowing this would be our last chance to add a child to our small family. I was already sad because now I would never fulfill my dream of having three children. I didn't think that I could handle a second miscarriage.

The thought terrified me. I didn't want another heartache.

After the embryo transfer, we waited two long weeks again for our beta. Three days before I was to have the blood work, I took a pregnancy test at home. It was negative. When going through IVF, the clinicians always tell patients *not* to perform a pregnancy test, but I wanted to know in that moment because Jeramy was traveling out of the country the next morning, and I wanted to be with him when I found out if I was pregnant or not. Deep down inside I was still sad, but I hadn't fully lost hope just yet.

An unexpected trip to the Dominican Republic had come up for Jeramy. His best friend, Matt, wanted him to travel to the town of Punta Cana with him. I was way jealous but so happy for him. He deserved a break. I couldn't go because, as a teacher, I can't take a week-long vacation during the school year; plus, I wanted to stay in town to receive my blood test results to learn whether or not I was pregnant. I was terrified by the thought of having to hear this news alone.

When Jeramy decided to go on vacation with his friend, we weren't thinking about all of the medications I was taking for IVF. I had to be given a progesterone shot each night, which is a shot administered in the upper buttocks and is very painful. It's a very thick gel-like shot, and there was no way I was going to be able to give this shot to myself. When I was pregnant with Preslee, I had to give myself a small shot in my stomach one day because Jeramy wasn't home. I had to lay on the bathroom floor afterward because I almost passed out. I knew there would be no way I could do this myself.

As I mentioned previously, Jeramy and I did not tell anyone that we were going through IVF again. We didn't want the heartache of having to explain to people that the procedure didn't work if it turned out I wasn't pregnant. However, because I needed this shot, I had no other choice but to tell someone, and it had to be someone who could give me these shots. We decided to tell my sister, Kayla. She was the only one I knew who would be able to stay with me for a whole week. I felt awful telling her before I had even told my mom, but I wanted it to be a surprise for my family. I also knew my mom would not be able to stay with me for an entire week to administer the shots. Kayla agreed to stay with me and give me the shots. Jeramy taught her how to give them correctly. I was terrified to have her give them to me, but I was desperate.

Jeramy left for Punta Cana, and my sister stayed with me. I was scared and frustrated that I might find out I wasn't pregnant and have to tell Jeramy while he was in a different country. I was also afraid that I would have to cope with a negative beta result alone. While I went to work, my sister stayed at my house and watched my daughter. I am so blessed to have a sister who was able and willing to help me through this. I knew my other sisters would gladly help as well, but one is a teacher who had to work and who also hates the thought of giving someone a shot. The other would have been very comfortable giving me shots because she works in an ob-gyn office, but she has two kids and also had to work, so she wouldn't have been able to stay with me either. The night before my beta test, Kayla convinced me to take another pregnancy test. I hesitantly did so, and to my surprise it was positive. I called Jeramy to let him know, while also reminding him that I shouldn't be taking pregnancy tests and that because of all the medications I was taking, the test could give a false positive.

Three days after Jeramy left for Punta Cana, the beta results came back positive! I tried to contain my excitement because I knew where that had gotten me the last time. Two days later, the results were still positive and my hCG levels had doubled! I couldn't believe it. I tried not to get too excited for fear of experiencing more heartache. I called Jeramy to let him know, and he was so happy. I was thankful to be able to give him this news because I knew he felt guilty about not being with me when I learned the results. I also did not want to ruin his vacation with a negative test result.

At six weeks pregnant, we went to our fertility clinic to get our first ultrasound. When the technician started the scan, we could see that the baby was growing like it should, but there was no heartbeat. My doctor told me that this is common and happens pretty frequently.

Sometimes the heart is not fully developed this early in the pregnancy. She scheduled us to come back in a week to complete another ultrasound.

Two nights later, my stomach felt funny. I went to use the restroom, and I started bleeding. There was so much blood. This had happened when I was six weeks pregnant with Preslee as well. But this time there was much more blood and clotting. I knew deep down that I had lost my baby. I was heartbroken when I called Jeramy into the restroom. I couldn't believe I was miscarrying again. I called my doctor after office hours to let her know. She told me that she would get me in first thing in the morning. I cried that entire night. I could barely sleep. I was sad for Preslee because I wanted her to have a brother or sister. I was also sad for myself because the one thing I wanted above all else was to be pregnant again. I was crushed.

The next morning we went back to the clinic, and my doctor started the ultrasound. Tears filled my eyes because I was afraid to face reality. Jeramy and I held hands. He softly stroked my hand to comfort me. I didn't want to look at the screen; instead, I stared at Jeramy. I could see fear in his eyes. The doctor did not say anything at first, which made me even more nervous. Then, *thump, thump, thump…* "There is your baby's heartbeat," she said. "Everything looks great. The baby has a very strong heartbeat. Your baby is fine. Looks like there is a small tear next to the sac, but fortunately, it is not right above the sac. Your baby is still growing and looks great! Congratulations!" Relief filled my body. I cried happy tears because I couldn't believe I didn't miscarry. Both Jeramy and I were relieved and excited to hear this news!

We decided to continue to keep my pregnancy a secret because we didn't want to have to explain why I was no longer pregnant if something did go wrong. We waited to tell anyone about it until I fell at work and could barely walk. The principal took me to the emergency room. I had to let the doctors there know that I was pregnant because they wanted to take an X-ray, and I didn't want my baby to be exposed to radiation. Fortunately, my foot was not broken, but I had to use crutches for a couple of weeks because I had sprained it so badly that I couldn't put weight on my foot. I called my mom to let her know that I was okay and, while telling her the story of what had happened, I accidently slipped and said I was pregnant. There was no way I could take those words back. I had wanted to surprise her but was still happy that she finally knew. Jeramy and I decided to let my dad and his parents know as well. Then, on Halloween, I announced it to my close family at my sister's Halloween party. I wore a shirt that pictured a baby skeleton on my stomach and just sat there until my sister noticed my shirt. Everyone was so excited. A few weeks later we decided to tell the rest of our family and friends since I was finally in the clear.

I was fearful throughout this pregnancy, afraid I
might miscarry again, but as the months passed, I
became more and more excited. Everything was going
well, although I did get a little nauseous with this baby. I
never had morning sickness during any of my
pregnancies but was pretty close with this one. I had to
go to labor and delivery at the hospital a couple of times
because I would get terrible headaches and become
dizzy. Each time I would be given fluids, but other than
that everything was going smoothly ... until my 26-week
ultrasound, which stole all of the excitement I had over
my final pregnancy.

Chapter 3
The Diagnosis Is Confirmed

"Something is wrong with your baby's heart," my ob-gyn doctor said at my 26-week ultrasound appointment. "We think she has Tetralogy of Fallot [a rare birth defect that affects normal blood flow through the heart]. The technician noticed that something was not right, which is why she asked you to wait for me."

My mind became a fog, and all I could muster was, "Is my baby going to die?" The doctor never gave me a direct answer; she did, however, call the fetal care team at our local hospital and ask them to squeeze us in to see their care team. We were quickly ushered out the back door so that we could avoid walking through the waiting room, where other parents might witness our distress. We were instructed to head straight to the hospital. Tears were rolling down my face faster than I could walk. Jeramy and I rushed to that hospital faster than anything. The car ride was silent. What do you even say when you get news like this? The entire way there I was researching the new medical term like crazy on my phone. I was trying to remember what the doctor had called our baby's condition. I knew it started with a "T," but everything felt like a blur.

When we arrived at the hospital, we had to check in and register. Preslee of course peed through her diaper, and Jeramy was in a panic. I could feel tension building up inside me. I felt myself shutting the world out, and I was getting annoyed at everything. I still held onto the hope that the substitute technician was wrong. I wanted nothing more than for her to be wrong. How can a substitute technician, who isn't even the regular one, be right? I felt angry and distraught.

I sat quietly in the waiting area for what felt like an eternity. When my name was finally called, I walked to the room as if I were walking to the gallows. It was at the end of a long hallway. Everyone who talked to me was smiling. I usually am always smiling, but I couldn't even put a fake smile on my face this time. I fought back my tears as I walked into the dark ultrasound room. The technician told me her name, but I honestly was not paying attention. I was meeting so many people so quickly, and I genuinely could care less what her name was at that time. I realized this was not her fault, but she's smiling at me. I felt this was no reason to smile, even though I knew she was just doing her job.

The warm gel was spread around my stomach. I again told the ultrasound technician that we did not know the gender of this baby and did not want to know. These were the only words I spoke during the entire ultrasound, which took over thirty minutes. The technician checked every little detail of our baby. She checked fluids, blood flow, the heart, length, weight, and so forth. I sat there very still, trying not to make a move and trying to shut my brain off. All I could do was stare at the monitor and think, how is this happening to me? How am I pregnant with my miracle rainbow baby, and now this baby may die? No one would answer that dreaded question, but realistically I don't think I really wanted to know the answer.

Jeramy tried so hard to entertain Preslee. My poor baby girl had enough of appointments for the day. She was tired and crabby. I was feeling like the worst mother in the world because I had yet to even feed her lunch. My stomach was in knots, my patience was at its wit's end, and my world was being shaken uncontrollably. The ultrasound technician finally finished. She handed me a few pictures of our baby, but I struggled to even look at them. She smiled and said the doctor would be in shortly.

The doctor walked in and said, "So, you were sent here by your ob-gyn because she suspects something is wrong with your baby's heart, correct?" Umm ... duh! is what I wanted to say to him, but instead I simply said yes. For a brief moment I could breathe. The way he spoke made me think for a slight second that my baby was healthy and this was all just some sort of mix-up. Then he uttered the next words that felt like a stab to my heart. "Well, your doctor was correct. Your baby has Tetralogy of Fallot. Meet Katie, she is going to help you organize your appointments and will stand by you throughout every step of the rest of your pregnancy. You are now considered a high-risk pregnancy. You will be followed by our care team very frequently." If my arm was long enough, I probably would have punched this doctor who was sitting across the room from me. His demeanor did not seem sincere. The way he came in and assaulted me with words that put false hope into my already broken heart just felt wrong.

I reached for my phone because my mom kept texting me. She knew that we had an ultrasound scheduled for today and realized that I was taking a long time to text her back. I didn't want to give her bad news over the phone, but I had to get back to her, and she is so perceptive at knowing when something is wrong. I texted my mom that the ultrasound was not going well. I explained how we are at the hospital now and just found out that our baby has a heart condition and, if we want the baby to live, it will need open-heart surgery as soon it's born. I said I didn't know much more than that but would contact her as soon as we left the hospital and let her know what we find out. I ended the text with, "We are going to see a fetal and pediatric cardiologist right now. No one is really telling us much. I am so afraid but will text you when I know more. I love you!"

She responded, "I am so sorry, baby girl. Call me when you leave." My heart was hurting and I was terrified.

Katie then walked me to the fetal and pediatric cardiologist, Dr. G. I was as nervous and scared as I could be. At the time, I never actually knew what a cardiologist was or what he did. I now know that *cardiologist* is the medical name for a heart doctor. I also never knew that a baby could have something wrong with its heart. Katie warned me that Dr. G is very quiet. She also said he is very good at what he does. She gave me a heads up that he would be very quiet during the ultrasound because he is very thorough and wants to make sure he is not missing anything. I was very happy she had warned me of this, because I was terrified and know I would have thought the worst. He planned to do the ultrasound first, followed by a fetal echocardiogram to study our baby's heart.

I laid on the table and lifted my shirt above my stomach. Dr. G came in and introduced himself to me. He looked at me for a slight second and patted my leg. He told me that I looked worried and scared and that my face was pale. He reminded me to breathe and assured me that no matter what he would take care of my baby. Then he started the fetal echocardiogram. It took everything I had in me to hold back the tears. I was overwhelmed. I was confused and in disbelief.

There was something about him, though, that made me believe what he said. I trusted that he would find out what was wrong with my baby's heart and know how to fix it. He warned me that some aspects of this ultrasound could hurt because he has to push down somewhat hard on my stomach. He told me that if I feel uncomfortable to let him know because he typically stares at the screen, so he isn't always aware that he is hurting me unless I say something. I would be lying if I said it did not hurt.

There was one point during the ultrasound when he was pushing down on my very sensitive belly button. It was so uncomfortable. I wanted to shout out how badly it was hurting. Instead I sat there quietly and did not utter a word. I was afraid to say something because I knew he needed to get these views of the baby's heart. I sat there very still and tried to distract my mind. Jeramy sat next to me and gently rubbed my hand while Preslee played with a few baby toys that were in the room. She was being so good. I kept staring at her, thinking how sad I would be for her to not have a sibling. After what seemed like a century, Dr. G finished his exam and walked us back to his office.

The office itself was not extraordinary. There was a small round table at which we were nervously sitting. His desk was positioned close to the table, and a stuffed bear, binders, books, and a couple of heart models lined the bookshelf behind it. Windows surrounded two of the walls, but they only provided a view of the hospital. His diplomas were hanging on the wall.

Katie entered the room, bringing with her a baggie of goldfish, chocolate chip cookies, and an apple juice for Preslee. She then sat in the chair to my left, between me and Dr. G. Preslee was sitting on my lap, and Jeramy was on my right. Dr. G pulled out a piece of paper with a black and white picture of a heart printed on it. When I used to think of hearts, I would picture a flat red shape with two humps at the top that flared out and down to form a point at the bottom. But Dr. G's picture did not look like that. It was a drawing of a heart, a real human heart organ. I honestly had never seen a picture like this one before.

Dr. G sat there and started to draw a picture of our baby's heart. He was not the best artist, and I was having a very difficult time imagining what it was he was trying to draw. Luckily, he was better at explaining than he was at drawing. He said that our baby has Tetralogy of Fallot with pulmonary atresia. He continued to draw, showing us how a normal heart looks: It has two separate ventricles (left and right) on the top and two separate ventricles on the bottom, as well as a pulmonary artery. He pointed to each area as he spoke. He then showed us how our baby's heart had a very large hole called a ventricular septal defect (VSD) in between the two lower chambers, causing a mix of blood. He explained how the baby's pulmonary artery was very short and narrow; it was practically closed. He said that on the ultrasound he could only see the smallest little trickle of blood passing through, practically none. He then went on to explain how this means our baby would need surgeries to fix its heart.

Because of the pulmonary atresia, our baby would require the services of a neonatal intensive care unit (NICU). Once born, the baby would go straight to the NICU to be placed on prostaglandins, which is a medicine that is administered through a central line to keep the pulmonary ductus open. The reason it needs to stay open is because its function is to take blood from the right ventricle and distribute it to the baby's lungs so the infant can breathe. If it were to close, it would cause a major catastrophe because the baby would not be able to breathe and would therefore die.

I tried to follow along with everything Dr. G was telling us. My heart felt like it was pounding through my chest. I felt ill. This was so much information to process, and I started to feel overwhelmed and confused. I tried very hard to hold back the tears, as I hate crying in front of people, but I couldn't help it. The tears continued to flow down my cheeks as I wiped them with a tissue. Jeramy asked some very good questions. Thank God he was with me because everything seemed like a fog. I struggled to digest all of the information that was put on the table in that moment. My world was spinning faster than I could keep up with. He explained that there was more to go along with this, but he did not want to completely overwhelm us. He was aware that it had been a long day for us and knew we needed time to process everything. His best advice that day was that we should not read about the baby's diagnosis on the internet because every case is different and we would only scare ourselves.

Dr. G gave us the names of four surgeons in our area to consider. We had to choose one of these because there were no other pediatric cardiovascular heart surgeons in the area. Two worked at one hospital and the other two at another. He told us to conduct some research and that the next time we meet he would tell us who he would suggest as the baby's heart surgeon. He also reassured us of his belief that with some research, we would likely choose the same surgeon he had in mind. We were given a binder in which the picture of our baby's heart was placed, along with contact information for him and Katie, a few brochures, and a notepad on which we could write down questions.

Jeramy and I left the appointment in a rush because his parents were already at our house waiting for us. We had planned for them to be in town this weekend to visit Preslee and us. Little did we know that this appointment would go the way it had gone. I was not in the mood to have visitors at the house. I was not ready to face reality or to pretend like everything was okay. I had recently started my dream job, and knowing that I would now have to miss a lot of work worried me. I desperately wanted this job and did not want to look undependable or irresponsible by missing so many days of work. I also didn't want my first graders to feel as though I was neglecting them, but I had no idea how to explain to anyone that my unborn baby had a broken heart and would need heart surgery within the first few days of life to stay alive. I was a mess.

I sent a text to the principal to let her know that our baby has something wrong with its heart and that I am now considered a high-risk pregnancy and therefore would miss a lot of work. She responded and told me to not even worry about work but to take care of myself and my baby. She assured me that my job would still be there for me, so I shouldn't worry about it. She has always believed that family needs to come first. It was reassuring to hear those things, but deep down I'm a worrier and missing work bugged me.

I was not sure how I was going to explain to family and friends that my baby has a congenital heart disease. I was confused myself, so how was I supposed to answer other people's questions? We decided to wait to tell anyone, other than our parents, until we understood more about our baby's heart ourselves. All four parents were very concerned but respected the fact that we still knew very little and could not provide any answers. My mom teaches medicine at a local college, but even she did not know much about pediatric heart problems. I was disappointed because I had always been able to call her in the past and ask her about medical concerns.

I was starting to feel more alone and scared than I have ever felt. I believed that no one would understand. I didn't know anyone who had a baby with a congenital heart defect (CHD). I also didn't know a thing about the heart other than it beats and is an important organ. How was I going to be a heart mom? How could I select a surgeon to perform surgery on my baby's heart and be able to trust this person? How was I going to spend an entire weekend with my in-laws, pretending as though life is okay, when in all actuality I felt like I was stuck in time and was suffocating?

Chapter 4
Going Through the Emotions

Throughout the rest of the pregnancy, I was tormented by stress and worry. Although I tried my best to prepare for what was to come, I soon realized that there really was no way to prepare for this. Because I was high-risk now, I needed to be seen weekly by the doctor for ultrasounds. The bad thing about weekly ultrasounds was that I would miss a lot of work and would have to travel over an hour both ways. The good thing about weekly ultrasounds was that I would get to see my baby every week, but not for the reasons I wanted. I felt like I had lost a part of me. I had trouble talking to others and started to distance myself from people and activities I had once enjoyed. All I wanted to do was love on Preslee. I wanted to spend every moment of every day with her as I became even more thankful to have her. I cherished every moment. I became very distracted at work and in everyday life, and I would constantly find myself lost in thought more often than I had before I received the bad news.

This whole process could either make or break me. For a while I chose to let it break me. I was falling apart. I had just miscarried before becoming pregnant with this baby. Here was my last chance to have another baby, and the thought that this baby could die after birth terrified me. I wanted to stay pregnant forever. I was continually reminded that as long as this baby is growing inside me, it is safe, and that the real worrying would begin after the baby is born. Naturally, I was terrified to give birth. The doctor said that after the baby is delivered, I could not hold it, it could not come home for a while, and it could not eat until after the first surgery. He tried to prepare me for the worst while at the same time reassuring me that everything would be okay. I didn't know what to think; my imagination was running wild.

After conducting extensive research, Jeramy and I were drawn to Dr. H. Everything we read about this surgeon was guiding us to him. We instinctively knew that he was the one who we could trust with our baby's heart. Thankfully, he also worked at the hospital we both went to as children, which was an enormous plus. We were scared to pick *any* surgeon, because it meant that no matter what happens, we might later regret having chosen that surgeon. When we told Dr. G our decision, he smiled and said, "Good, that is who I was hoping you would select. Both surgeons at that hospital are amazing. No matter what happens, your baby will be in experienced hands. They both are outstanding cardiovascular heart surgeons. When you put them together, you couldn't ask for a better team." We were relieved and confident that we had chosen the surgeon who Dr. G would have suggested.

Over the next few weeks we went to a lot of appointments. Katie was awesome at scheduling them for me and keeping me updated throughout this whole ordeal. I spent the next few weeks researching the baby's condition, visiting the NICU at both hospitals, and touring the Pediatric Intensive Care Unit (PICU), as well as meeting with the baby's heart surgeon about open-heart surgery and the steps the surgeons would take to repair our baby's heart. I felt like I was on information overdrive. It was a lot to take in and somewhat impossible to process it all.

They told us that our baby's diagnosis could stem from a genetic condition, possibly DiGeorge Syndrome, 22q11 deletion. The symptoms include congenital heart defects, learning problems, cleft palate, special facial features, and frequent infections. They asked if we wanted to have genetic testing performed. We knew that no matter what was wrong with our baby, we would love him or her. Knowing if our baby has this condition before we give birth would not change anything, so we opted out of genetic screening. It was difficult not knowing, but if our baby did have this funny-sounding condition, I didn't want to be stressed trying to learn about it as well. To say I was feeling overwhelmed would be an understatement.

Jeramy and I started to see things differently. At work I was able to hide my fears and emotions, but at home I wore them on my sleeve. I was constantly talking about this baby and my fears regarding its health. My husband would not talk much about it and had little desire to listen to me. I felt like I was talking to a brick wall. I would talk, and he would semi-listen but not respond. The few times he did respond were to tell me that the baby would be fine, which only served to make me even angrier, although I kept it inside. I was getting tired of the lie. I was frustrated by everyone trying to tell me that everything is going to be okay. They had no way of knowing this, and it was not what I wanted to hear. I honestly have no idea what I wanted to hear, but a part of me just wanted to know that someone understood what I was feeling. I felt as if I had no one on my side. Not one person understood what I was going through. I was in this alone.

I know my husband was scared, but the fact that he didn't want to talk about it infuriated me inside. A fire was lit that couldn't be put out. Our baby's diagnosis was taking over my life and consumed my every thought. I was struggling to sleep, and when I did fall asleep, I would have nightmares about what was going to happen with the baby. I began to hide my feelings in the one place I always thought I wouldn't have to … in my own home. I learned to put on my fake smile and move on with life. I struggled with my identity; I didn't know who I was anymore. I constantly researched medical terms and conditions. I cried when I was alone. I hid my feelings and faked my emotions. I started to do something that was only hurting myself: I started to remain silent.

As the weeks came and went, I became more and more terrified of what was to come. I tried to lie to myself and tell myself that everything would be fine and that I would be fine too. Hiding my feelings worked for a while, but it erected a barrier between my marriage and the people closest to me. I became easily irritated, avoided people and activities that I loved, and focused primarily on Preslee and spoiling her. I started spending money that I didn't have, with the thought that I would buy Preslee everything she wanted simply because she deserves it. I intended to live life to the fullest by granting her every wish (more like what I wished for her). I pampered my daughter because buying Preslee happiness helped to bring me temporary happiness and gave me a reason to smile. Although, in hindsight, it actually caused bigger problems because we were already struggling financially after having gone through IVF three times. We also needed to save money for our new baby's arrival. The money problems caused even more arguments between me and Jeramy.

I started to dislike my life, and I didn't like myself either. I didn't want to talk to anyone. I no longer wanted to give birth to this baby because I couldn't face the harsh reality that our child might have serious health problems. I wanted to stay pregnant forever. After much brooding, however, I accepted that I had no control over the situation. I had to let it go. I had to find a way to be okay with not being okay.

I met another heart mom, who I'll call Loretta, for privacy sake. Her son has the same condition as my baby. She shared pictures of her son with me throughout his surgeries and recovery. She gave me hope that everything would be okay. I talked to her often, and any time I had a question I went to her. She talked to me about my financial fears, my motherly fears, and overall life with a CHD child. She and her son were doing well, which made me hope and believe that my baby and I would be okay too. She gave me a newfound confidence that I had been sorely lacking.

Loretta told me about everything she had gone through to pay for her son's surgeries and treatment. She had applied to the state for financial aid. Because she wasn't married yet, the processor looked solely at her income, rather than hers and the baby's father, to determine whether or not she qualified for benefits and, if so, how much money she was eligible to receive. I decided to apply to the state for help in paying for our baby's expenses. I was a little hopeful that I would receive financial aid because my baby has a life-threatening condition; it simply would not be able to live without surgery. We have health insurance, but it's not the best; our deductibles and out-of-pocket expenses are outrageously high. After waiting for over a month to find out if I had qualified, I received notification that I was not eligible for financial aid because my income is too high. This is something of which I am proud, considering I worked hard to get where I am today, but how is a working person who makes a small salary supposed to afford a deductible that is so high?

Not qualifying for financial aid threw me into a deeper depression. How could I ever afford to have a heart baby? How would I have the funds to buy anything for my babies when every dollar is going to pay hospital bills? All of this was becoming too much to bare. I was terrified, absolutely dumbstruck about how I was going to stay afloat. More and more things kept piling up. The bills started to stack up. I was missing work and taking unpaid personal days for appointments and other dealings with the baby. I had to stop buying Preslee things (which was probably for the better), but buying things for her was therapeutic for me. Now I had no other outlet.

Jeramy and I did not see eye to eye when it came to our baby's diagnosis, which I contribute largely to his growing up with cystic fibrosis. He had beaten the odds since day one. I have never had to suffer from a chronic illness before, or the physical suffering and pain that go along with it, whereas he was of the mindset, "It is what it is, and it will be fine." I didn't see it that way. I knew I couldn't change my baby's diagnosis, and it was eating me up inside. I had an X-ray when I was only a few weeks along in the pregnancy and wondered if the radiation had somehow caused the baby's problems. Maybe it was my fault. Did I do something wrong to be given a heart baby? I blamed myself and took it out on the people I loved the most because I didn't know how else to handle the situation.

We eventually announced our baby's diagnosis to all of our family and friends. We finally felt comfortable enough to answer some of those dreaded questions we knew would come. Of course, there were lots and lots of questions. There was also an outpouring of support that we desperately needed. The day was April 4, 2017. April is also infertility month. I logged into Facebook and wrote:

"In honor of infertility month! This is my little peanut. (I attached a picture of her profile ultrasound picture with all the needles from IVF placed around it in the shape of a heart lying on a blanket that reads, 'God Knew My Heart Needed You.') Those of you who are close to me know how much I have always wanted to be a mommy.

Jeramy and I chose to do IVF to start a family. Having only 3 embryos fertilize, we chose to implant one and freeze the other 2 in hopes of having three babies. First cycle was a success, and we now have our amazing baby girl, Preslee Wilson. We tried again, and it worked, but we shortly after miscarried, for only reasons God knows. We asked ourselves what do we have to lose? And tried with our last frozen embryo back to back. Theses needles aren't even all of the shots and medicines I had to use/do to get pregnant, but it was worth all the pokes, bleeds, and pains. We are now almost 31 weeks along. Although this pregnancy hasn't seemed fair and has caused me a lot of worries and fears, I am so blessed to get to be this baby's mommy. We found out at 26 weeks that this little peanut has a heart condition called Tetralogy of Fallot with Pulmonary Atresia. We are seeing a specialist weekly now to make sure this baby gets all the care it needs when born. He/she will undergo 2 heart surgeries, once when born and another around 6 months. I'm only making this post to make people aware of the struggle a lot of people go through! I have come to realize that things could always be worse! Be thankful for what God gives you. If there is one thing I have learned through this journey is to never take anything for granted."

Little did I know at the time that there was so much more to this journey, and that God was about to really put me to the test.

48

We decided that when it was time for me to deliver, we would not announce it to anyone. We did not want the burden of having to answer a thousand questions, give updates, and explain to the world what happened if everything did not go as planned. On May 30, I went to my 37-week checkup with my ob-gyn, and then with our fetal care team. Things got crazy, and my whirlwind of emotions began to spiral.

Chapter 5
Baby Day

    The day started off pretty normal. I went to my 37-week ob-gyn appointment. I was only one centimeter dilated and was experiencing Braxton Hicks contractions. My baby was positioned with its head down and had a good heartbeat. The plan was to hold off on delivery as long as possible so that our baby could gain weight. Babies with CHD tend to be on the smaller side, and the bigger the better. After the appointment, my doctor and I finished up, and she said she would see me next week. Off to the fetal care appointment and ultrasound I went.

    The office was very busy that day. They decided to perform my stress test first. Preslee sat in the room with me and played with her game. She was being extra cute that day and was on her best behavior for the appointment. The stress test was recording a lot of contractions, and our baby seemed to be doing well. We finally went in for the ultrasound. I, of course, received a lot of pictures of our baby. It's funny, because on every ultrasound, our baby tends to hide its face with her leg. We always joke around about how this baby is going to be a gymnast. The ultrasound was complete, and nothing seemed out of the ordinary. The doctor came in and sat down. She said, "I think it's baby day. I am concerned with the growth of your baby. Each week our baby falls further and further behind in percentiles. She is no longer growing, your fluids are on the lower side, and I think we should induce you and meet this baby. What do you think?"

I was nervous, but whatever was best for my baby is what I wanted. They called my ob-gyn, who said she does inductions on Wednesdays. Fortunately, today was Tuesday, so scheduling would not be a problem. The doctor reassured me that this was the best decision. She stated that everyone would be present at the induction who needed to be, including the NICU doctor and the hospital cardiologist. She smiled and said, "Go home and pack your bags. We'll be calling you shortly to tell you when to come in."

I left the appointment terrified, but I was also excited to finally meet this baby. I called Jeramy to let him know it was "go" time. He left work and met me at home. We let our parents know and grabbed our bags. My parents are more than amazing and were willing to watch Preslee and even our dog for us. Okay, maybe they weren't happy about watching our dog (because my mom hates dogs), but they would do whatever they needed to do for me. I thank God all the time for my parents. We dropped Preslee and the dog off to them and away we went. We grabbed dinner and then headed to the hospital. When we arrived, we went straight to the labor and delivery area, registered, and waited to go up to our room. I had delivered Preslee naturally, so I was even more terrified of the induction, which would be another "first" for me. I had never been induced before, so I didn't know what to expect. Everything in my life seemed to be going this way lately.

When we got to the room, the nurse placed an IV in my arm. She explained that this would be a very slow process because the doctor didn't want me to have this baby until tomorrow, when everyone who would be involved was ready. She reminded me to get some rest so that I would be ready for labor the next morning. Ha, I couldn't help but laugh, thinking to myself, so you want me to get rest? Do you know that I am about to have a heart baby? And you expect me to relax? This was never going to happen. That night I was exhausted but couldn't sleep. All of my fears were starting to become a reality. I could not wait to discover if I was having a boy or girl, but I wasn't ready to find out yet. I was too terrified.

At 4 am, my mom and sister decided to surprise me at the hospital. My mom brought Preslee with her. I was a little annoyed because I just wanted a minute to myself to focus on what was going on. Preslee was so exhausted and tired; I wished they would have stayed home and let her sleep—or at the very least, let me know ahead of time that they were coming so I could have found someone else to care for her that night. I didn't want her to be stuck at the hospital all day. Plus, I had other things to worry and stress about.

I understood that my mom wanted to be there simply because she is my mom and that's what moms do. And I wanted her to be there, I honestly did, but I hated that my toddler was there, and I hated even more that she was so crabby. My mom thought Preslee would stay asleep, but I knew better. It was sort of nice to have my sister and mom there though. Jeramy was sleeping, and I needed the comfort of having someone with me to distract me from the stark reality that was about to happen. So even though I was a little annoyed, deep down I was thankful to not be alone.

At 7 am, one of my sisters dropped off her two daughters to my mom because she watches them during the day in the summer. This brought even more chaos to the room. Preslee was crabby, her cousins were hyper, the room was loud, and I was overwhelmed. I had too much on my plate, and I was reaching my boiling point. My family tried hard to keep the kids entertained, but that's impossible when they are stuck in a hospital room. I had been so overwhelmed throughout this entire pregnancy, and I'm sure my stress did not help my levels of patience and understanding. I wanted to cry. The day was not going as planned, just like everything else in my life. I threw up a few times while contracting. I had done this with Preslee as well, and it is the worst feeling. I was shaking like crazy as well. The nurse said this is normal, that the epidural and all the medicines I had taken can cause the shaking. I felt miserable.

Around 10 am it was time for me to start pushing. My epidural had worn off, and I was in so much pain I could barely stand it. I was begging the nurses to give me more pain medicine, but they couldn't, due to the fact that it could slow the delivery. I didn't care; the pain was so bad that I struggled to push. This was nothing like my delivery with Preslee. All I had felt with her was pressure. With this delivery all I felt was pain. I lost faith in myself. I didn't think I could do it. My ob-gyn was not there yet, so a nurse called the on-call doctor to come in. Why is this happening to me? Why is another thing not going as planned? I can't do this. It doesn't feel right. Unfortunately, I had no choice. Everyone was supposed to be here, so why isn't everyone here? This is the reason why I am being induced. I grew more and more terrified as time passed.

While pushing, my baby's heart rate dropped significantly low. I began to panic. I was instructed to stop pushing and to lay on my right side. An oxygen tube was placed on me, and nurses were rubbing my stomach, trying to get my baby's heart rate back up.

I was then told to turn on my left side, where

nurses again pushed on my stomach and tried to get my baby's heart rate up. Nothing was working. By the grace of God, Katie walked in at that moment. I remember looking at Jeramy and seeing fear in his eyes. I looked over at Katie, and she grabbed my hand. She said I looked as though I needed someone to hold my hand. Boy, was she right. I don't think she will ever know how badly I needed her at that moment. The on-call doctor showed me a vacuum and explained how it would be used. At this point, my ob-gyn finally arrived. She said she would work together with the on-call doctor to pull my baby out. I was informed that there are risks associated with it but was assured that the benefits far outweigh the risks. I had no time to even consider the risks. My baby had to be delivered immediately. Its life depended on it. The on-call doctor quickly placed the vacuum on the top of my baby's head and instructed me to push while he pulled our baby out.

Jeramy said, "It's a girl!" I could not believe what I had just heard. I was convinced that we were having a boy, so that announcement really threw me for a loop. But the one thing I didn't hear was baby cries. I thought, why isn't she crying? Is she okay? I looked down and the on-call doctor was holding this blue baby by her foot and rubbing her back. The room was silent. I was in a panic. Then, the beautiful soft cries of a newborn baby filled the room. They were very silent cries, but they were cries just the same. The NICU nurses took her and quickly listened to her heart and cleaned her airway, then they made her footprint and weighed her. She was 5 pounds, 10 ounces. A beautiful, nameless baby girl. They showed her to me for a few seconds. I was able to kiss her little cheek, and then off she went to the NICU.

In that moment I felt as though everything had been stolen from me. I did not get to enjoy my last pregnancy, have a normal delivery, or most importantly, hold my baby and have her little body placed on my chest to begin establishing our mother/daughter bond right away. I did not get to nurse my baby or truly see her. Jeramy went downstairs with Preslee, while I stayed upstairs to be monitored and spruced up.

Jeramy came back upstairs about thirty minutes later and showed me pictures of our beautiful baby girl. I felt like I was dying inside. The room was full of my family: my other daughter, my husband, my grandma, my sisters ... but I felt alone, very alone and sad. All I wanted was to be with my newborn daughter. I couldn't stand the fact that she was downstairs having a central line and a peripherally inserted central catheter (PICC) line placed into her tiny body so that she could survive. I hated that I was not by her side, loving on her and letting her know that her mommy was there. I had to trust people I had just met that day to keep her alive.

Waiting to see my baby girl gave me a lot of time to think. Everything about this pregnancy was so different from my pregnancy with Preslee. I never got to enjoy being pregnant because I was terrified of the "what ifs." I wasn't given the opportunity to go into labor on my own; I had to be induced. I wasn't allowed to push my baby out; she had to be pulled out. I didn't get to hold her; she was rushed to the NICU so she could live. I didn't get to feel the immense joy that a mom feels just being pregnant and knowing she's going to have a baby. All I had was fear. I was still terrified, maybe even more so now that I had met my baby, and I was falling apart inside. I was convinced that the world was against me and my baby.

The day after I delivered Preslee, I remember the photographer at the hospital coming in to take pictures of her. They were beautiful. This time, no photographer would be showing up. Newborn pictures couldn't be taken until she was able to leave the hospital—and who knows how long that would be. I was crushed inside. I would not enjoy the luxury of having my baby wheeled into my room so I could feed her and love on her. I couldn't experience the pleasure of hearing and responding to her cries because she was on oxygen, which made her cries sound silent. I would have to wait to show her off to our friends and family and let them hold her and have their pictures taken with her, because she was now confined to a bed. I wouldn't be able to breastfeed her because it would be too hard on her heart, and she wasn't allowed to eat. I was useless.

Three long, painful hours went by before I was finally wheeled down to the NICU. They showed me how to get to her room. I stood up and stared at my beautiful newborn baby girl, who was hooked to an oxygen tank, had monitors on her stomach, a pulse oximeter reader on her wrist, IVs, and a central line in her now bloody and stitched belly button. They explained to me that the pulse oximeter was a machine that would continuously let us know her heart rate and oxygen levels. If levels became too low or high, it would sound the alarms.

I stared at the monitor that showed me my daughter's heartbeat was abnormal. The lines representing her heartbeat were all over the place. This is what is called a "brady," which is short for bradycardia, a slower than normal heart rate. I watched as red lights and an obnoxious sound would alarm us every time her heart rate dropped. It took everything in me not to collapse on that floor and lose it. But now was the time I had to be strong. I needed to be brave for my family and for my new baby. I must hide my emotions and learn to pretend to be okay.

I stood in that room and refused to let anyone push me around in a wheelchair. I was in pain, I was hurting, and I couldn't sit comfortably. I had just given birth after all, but I was not going to baby myself or allow anyone else to either. I did not want to leave her side, and I was not about to be wheeled around only because I was in pain. I looked at my beautiful daughter and thought, how can I complain about pain? How can I be babied? This beautiful baby is fighting harder than anyone I have ever met, and there is no way that I would allow anyone to focus on babying me. I'll suck it up and act fine because my daughter needs my attention and my strength, and I'll do whatever it takes to give her both.

I walked to my room so I could get organized and pump my breast milk. My two nieces, daughter, sisters, two nephews, grandma, and mom were in the small room with us. Preslee and her two cousins were all worked up. They had been at the hospital all day, which seems like forever to kids so young. They took the wheelchair that I had refused to sit in and went to play with it in the hallway. They were so worked up and hyper, pushing the wheelchair into walls and making a lot of noise. I couldn't blame them, but I was overwhelmed. There was too much going on. I just wanted to be alone and cry my eyes out, but people were everywhere.

One nurse came in and told us that people were complaining about the noise level in our room, so we would need to lower our voices. I was so emotional that I took it to heart. I felt bad for my mom because she wanted to stay with me, but she had to babysit my nieces and Preslee, so in order for her to be there, they had to be there too. I was on overdrive, and everything was starting to bug me. I just wanted to be in the room with my baby. Only two people could go back at a time to visit her, and I wanted to let my family see her while they were there. She looked so tiny in that bed, with IVs and lines decorating her body.

In this moment, our lives changed forever. Depression, loneliness, and sadness were filling my body. I watched my baby girl fight big battles that day. I started to drift further away from the people who had come to be there for me. No one understood how I felt, not even my husband. I hid those feelings like I had learned to do so well over the past few months.

I became more and more distraught because of the situation and my husband's attitude toward it. I was angry at him. How could he not want to be in this room with our daughter 24/7? How could he expect me to come back to my "room"? I didn't want to leave her; how could he? We, in this moment, did not understand each other. We were coping in completely different ways. This would soon lead me to a darker path. When I wasn't with my baby, I was pumping breast milk or eating. I produced a lot of milk, and it saddened me that I had to put it into a freezer instead of into my baby's stomach. As the days went on, the walls were caving in on me. I became obsessed with researching my baby's condition and pumping. I distanced myself from the outside world and focused solely on my baby.

Two days later, Jeramy and I came to an agreement on what to name our baby. We decided to name her Lillian Eileen Wilson. I was so excited that we had finally agreed on a name, because now I could call her something other than mommy's baby girl, and the hospital staff would no longer have to refer to her as Baby Girl Wilson. We also were told that the genetic screening showed Lillian did not have DiGeorge Syndrome, so that was a huge relief. Jeramy wanted me to come back to the room with him so that I could finally get some much-needed rest. I know he was only trying to look out for me and make sure I was taking care of myself, but I didn't want him to do anything for me. I wanted him to leave me alone and just let me do what I wanted to do. I didn't want to be babied. I didn't want someone looking out for me. I wanted everyone to focus their love and attention on Lillian.

That night, when he fell asleep, I walked into Lillian's room and broke down. I lost it. I stared at my baby girl sucking on a little green binky that looked way too big in her little mouth, and I was angry. I was angry at God, angry at myself, and angry with my life. This was not fair for my baby girl. Lillian didn't ask for this life and neither did I. I was supposed to have a healthy baby. No, I was supposed to have three healthy babies. I wasn't supposed to miscarry, and I wasn't supposed to have a baby with a broken heart. I laid on the small couch that was in the room, curled myself into a ball, and cried while staring at her alarm monitor until I finally drifted off to sleep. I wanted so badly to wake up and find out this was all just a nightmare. But it was not a bad dream. It was now my reality ... and my life.

That day I became a true heart mom. I wasn't quite ready to accept this title, but it wasn't about me, and I didn't have a choice. I was determined to do whatever needed to be done to bring Lillian home with me. I learned everything I needed to learn. I wanted to make sure I understood all that she was going through. I shut out the world around me and concentrated on Lillian. She and Preslee were all that mattered to me. I knew that Preslee would be okay with our parents, so I had to focus solely on Lillian. In that moment my precious newborn baby girl needed me the most.

Chapter 6
Off to the Next Hospital

On June 2, 2017, it was finally time for Lillian to go to the next hospital. I was excited for this transfer because we would be going to the facility at which Lillian's heart surgeon and team worked. I was so ready to go to a hospital where I was confident that the doctors and staff are well prepared to take care of her and her heart. On transfer day I packed all of our things. I also made sure that I, too, was discharged on this day so that I could go to the hospital with Lillian. I was kind of sad that someone had thrown away the hat that was placed on her right after she was born. I had kept the hat given to Preslee at her birth for a keepsake, and now I would never have one for Lillian. But, as Jeramy would say, "It is what it is." A nurse put Lillian in a different bed and then gathered an oxygen tank, a respiratory bag, and all of my frozen breast milk. Jeramy and my sister, Kayla, rode to the next hospital together, while I rode in the ambulance with Lillian.

During the ride to the new hospital, the nurses and the emergency medical technician (EMT) who traveled with us talked a lot. I was still super emotional, and to be honest, I don't remember much of what they said. Lillian started to spit up, but the EMT nurse didn't notice and continued to talk to me. I was livid. I looked at her and said, "My daughter is spitting up, and she appears to be choking!" She hurried and stuck a red tube in Lillian's nose to clear her airway. She called it a "red rubber." I was trying not to snap inside. How could she be so careless? How did she not notice this? I continued to breathe, as I just wanted to hurry up and get to the hospital.

We finally arrived, and I followed behind as the EMT wheeled her in. We made our way to the NICU. The small room was packed. People were everywhere, working to get Lillian transferred to her new bed. They took off her oxygen tube and hooked her up to what is called a bubble continuous positive airway pressure (CPAP). I didn't have a clue what this was; it was explained to me that it is similar to oxygen but is easier on the baby and helps to keep her airways open. I was so happy that we were finally at this hospital. Lillian was hooked up to a pulse oximeter, which measures oxygen saturation of a patient's blood, and for the first time, her heart was not bradying every minute. She seemed more comfortable, and so did I. I finally felt like I could breathe (just a little) again.

The room was very small, and to top it off, we were right above the floor that uses radiation, so we had absolutely no cellular service to contact anyone. This really took a toll on me, because having no phone service completely disconnected me from the outside world. The only time I left Lillian's room was when I had to use the restroom or grab something to eat from the cafeteria. Not being able to receive or make phone calls or texts made me feel even more distant and alone. The "bed" that Jeramy and I had to sleep on was a very tiny couch that did not fold out into a bed. It was more like a loveseat. There was no television. Luckily, we were able to connect to Wi-Fi, so I was able to use Facebook to communicate when needed.

For the first two days, Lillian was in the NICU. We arrived at the hospital on a Friday, but the cardiology team wouldn't meet to discuss their heart patients and formulate plans until Monday. Therefore, all we needed to do for the next couple of days was to keep her stable. I felt sad that I was not able to feel like a mother to my newborn baby. I was not able to hold my baby, feed her, soothe her, or even change her diapers.

What type of new mom am I? Well, I am a heart mom. And as I've said before, I was not ready for this journey, although I don't feel anyone is ever truly ready. This did not help at all to ease my depression. I felt useless. All I could do was pump and freeze, pump and freeze, pump and freeze, until I felt like a cow in a milk factory. I could rub Lillian's head and talk to her, which I did constantly. When she cried, I could put her binky in her mouth. That's about all I could do, but at least it was something.

Each day the NICU team and the cardiology team would make their rounds and talk about Lillian. "This is Lillian. She arrived here on June 2. She is a tet baby. Blood count is fine, oxygen is low…" Then they would enter the room and listen to her heart, ask us if we had any questions, and then quietly leave and make their way to the next room.

On June 4 we were assigned a lovely nurse named Tara. She was the first nurse to write Lillian's name on the door. She placed a little pink bow she had made on Lillian's head. She was the sweetest lady I had met there so far. She talked to me about her family and children and how proud she was of them. She spoke to Lillian as though my baby was more than just a heart baby stuck to a bed. Tara was gentle, genuine, and sweet.

She asked if I had changed my baby's diaper yet, and when I told her no, she let me help change Lillian. While I was changing her, she peed on me and then started to poop. Never have I been happier to be peed and pooped on than in that moment. Tara then asked the one question I had been waiting to be asked since my baby was born, which caused me to choke up and want to cry. She asked me if I had held Lillian yet. My response was, "No, because I was told that I couldn't."

Tara smiled at me and said, "Today you are going to hold your baby." It took everything in me not to cry my eyes out in that very moment. Tara told me she has been a nurse for a long time. She knows how to be careful with a heart baby, and she understands that a mom *needs* to hold her baby. She asked me to sit in a chair, and she placed a white pillow on my lap. It took her awhile to carefully move all of the wires and tubes out of the way, but she eventually did and placed Lillian on my lap.

In that moment, life stood still. Nothing else mattered. After five long days, Lillian was in my arms. I was finally able to hold my pretty baby. Tara said Lillian was beautiful. She told me that she doesn't ask for permission but instead asks for forgiveness. She was my angel sent from God, who must have known how sad and disconnected I was becoming. I truly believe that he sent Tara to me to remind me that I am a mother and, although this whole experience is new to me, I will survive, I will be okay, and I will always understand and appreciate how much Lillian needs me. I can never thank this beautiful angel nurse enough. I cried while I was holding Lillian. I never wanted the moment to end. Tara allowed me to hold her for a while. She checked on us constantly to make sure we were okay. She eventually had to place Lillian back in her bed, even though I didn't want to let my baby go, but I was so thankful for the short period of time I was given to connect with my newborn daughter. I needed it so much.

That night my sister, Jessica, and my mom were in the room with Lillian and me. A chaplain walked in and asked if he could pray with us. I am not a super religious person. I believe in God, although I don't attend church on a regular basis. Some might frown on this, but Lillian has brought me closer to God. I am trying my best to be a better person and mother and am confident I will be. I will allow anyone to pray for Lillian because I pray for her constantly myself. I don't see any harm in it.

The chaplain asked me if I believed in God. I quickly replied, "Absolutely." He asked if I currently attend a church, and I explained to him that I am a believer but do not attend church regularly. He asked what religion I was associated with. I was thrown off by all of the questions. I meant to answer, "Christian," but I accidently said "Catholic." Now how on Earth do I take that back? Was I supposed to say, "No, just kidding, I am Christian"? So, I just went with what I had said.

He asked if I wanted to lead us in prayer. I quickly looked at my sister, Jessica, who is very religious and attends church on a regular basis. I quickly replied with, "My sister would love to pray." If looks could kill, I would have been dead in that moment.

Jessica pointed to herself and said, "Me? NO, thank you. You can go ahead and say the prayer." At this point all of us were trying so hard not to laugh. Jessica is Baptist, not Catholic, and there is a huge difference. We were not trying to be rude or disrespectful to the chaplain and especially toward God. But I could not take back what I had said, and I know very little about being a Catholic.

The chaplain led the prayer, and we all prayed along with him. I kept thinking about how dumb I was to tell the chaplain that I was Catholic. In my mind I kept replaying what had just happened and was doing everything in my power not to bust out laughing about the situation. Afterwards, I thanked him for praying with us for Lillian. When he left the room, we all burst into laughter. My sister thanked me for putting her on the spot like that. Hahaha, I needed that laugh so badly.

Sunday rolled around, and doctors made their rounds to check on Lillian. They asked if I had been given the opportunity to hold Lillian yet. I didn't want to get Tara in trouble, so I said no. They expressed their concern that Lillian needs to be held more often and told me to ask a nurse whenever I wanted to hold her. They had nothing new to report, which is code for, "Your baby is currently doing better than all of the other heart babies, so all is well."

I held Lillian on and off that day, and Jeramy was able to finally hold her. It's crazy that we had to ask someone to help us hold our own daughter, but she had very important and necessary lines going into her body, and we couldn't chance tugging on them. The smallest mistake could be deadly to Lillian. We were scared but so happy to be holding her. I also got to change a poopy diaper. It's weird, but I have never been happier to change a diaper in my life. I was starting to somewhat feel as though I wasn't so useless. I could start to do some mommy things, which helped me cope a little bit. But then Monday rolled around, and reality was about to smack me in the face again. I was definitely not ready for Monday.

Chapter 7
Time for Surgery

Monday morning finally arrived. Jeramy and I were anxious to hear what the cardiology team had discussed during their meeting. We would now be told about their plans to treat Lillian. It seemed as though we had spent the past three days just laying around waiting and making no progress. I guess you could say we were more than ready for a surgery date to be set. I kind of wanted to just get the surgery over with but was terrified at the same time.

Lillian's heart surgeon, Dr. H, entered our room around 11:15 am. He said good morning and made small talk with us. Then he cut straight to the chase. "So, we discussed Lillian's case this morning, and she seems to be doing well. Our schedule is booked this whole week with surgeries that need to take place." At this point I started to feel discouraged. Please do not tell me that we have to wait another week for her surgery. Then he continued, "However, we had an appointment cancellation for today; therefore, we can perform her surgery today. It will start at 12 pm if that is okay with you."

Jeramy and I both looked at each other. "Do you think you know enough about Lillian that you are well prepared to perform her surgery this quickly?" I asked. Dr. H said yes, that he was ready. We both agreed that if the surgeon felt confident, we could trust him.

The nurse asked me if I wanted to quickly hold Lillian while we waited for someone from the anesthesia team to come in and talk to us. She placed Lillian in my arms, and I broke down. I finally cried in front of other people. As much as I wanted this to be over with, I was terrified. What if this is the last time I will get to see my baby alive? What if I never get to hold her again? Then I started crying uncontrollably while staring at my one-week-old baby girl. I cried and cried and cried and then cried some more.

Jeramy said he wanted to take a picture of me holding Lillian, but I looked terrible. I couldn't stop the tears from falling down my cheeks. I could not believe that I had only fifteen minutes to prepare for this surgery. As much as I wanted this to be over with, all I really wanted to do was unhook Lillian from all of these machines and run away with her. I wanted to hide her away from the world. Truth be told, I was a chicken and would never be prepared for this. I wanted to throw up. I couldn't help but think that this could be my last opportunity to have my picture taken with Lillian. I know that was not the right attitude, but I couldn't help feeling this way. Fear was filling my mind. I didn't want this to be my last moment with her. It was a sad moment. I was crying, I was scared, I had bad thoughts running through my mind, and I felt helpless. I needed for there to be more after this. I prayed there would be a light at the end of this tunnel, and I would get a call telling me that Lillian had made it out of surgery and had done well. But thinking about the wait and how long we might be stuck "not knowing," did not help comfort me.

A lady from the anesthesia team came in and asked us to sign a consent form, allowing her to put Lillian under during the surgery. It was so hard to sign that paper. The nurse entered the room and asked if I was ready. Is that even a real question? I will never be ready, but what choice do I have? I looked at Lillian's chest. Her soft newborn skin looked perfect. I rubbed my hand over her body but couldn't help to think that this is the last time we will ever see her without scars. Her beautiful skin, so soft, smooth, and perfect, would soon be covered in bandages and blood, and she will have earned her first scar. She would never again be scar free. She would earn her first beauty mark of strength and survival.

I kissed Lillian's little lips, tiny hands, and chest and then handed her to the nurse, and she placed her

73

back in her bed. Handing her over to someone else was so hard. I have always been so good at appearing "strong" and keeping myself together in front of people, but this time I wasn't managing so well. The surgery team came in and told us to give her our hugs and kisses and promised that they would take great care of her. All I could think was, *they better*. Jeramy kissed Lillian on the cheek, but I just couldn't bring myself to do it. I couldn't say goodbye. I had already told my baby that I was fine when I had last held her. Jeramy and I went into the hallway to give everyone some space. I cried in Jeramy's arms as they wheeled Lillian into the elevator and headed to surgery. And just like that, I was standing in a hallway looking into an empty NICU room, knowing that we would never be back in that room. What if this is the last moment I will ever have to see Lillian alive? I felt numb. My body was aching. I felt so cold when I looked into that empty room. I was already regretting not having kissed my beautiful baby just one more time.

The nurses instructed Jeramy and I to take our bags upstairs to the second floor. They explained that we would check in with surgery and then go next door to the PICU. They informed us that staff would most likely have a room set up for us because they are already prepared for Lillian to go there after surgery. Jeramy and I headed upstairs and let surgery know that our daughter had just been taken back to the operating room.

The receptionist in the surgery waiting area was

confused and did not know Lillian had already been taken back. We asked if we could go to the PICU to check in. I needed to pump, and we also needed somewhere to place our belongings. I picked up the black phone hanging on the wall in the PICU. We were told that the door to the PICU is always locked, and in order to get back there, we had to be buzzed in.

I explained to the lady who I am and who my daughter is. Again, another confused person who acted as though she had no idea we were there, and why on earth would they would tell us that there would be a room available for us? I started to become agitated. This was not something that I wanted to deal with. I had enough on my plate. My daughter had just been wheeled back to receive her first heart surgery. I am terrified and emotional, and yet no one seems to know a thing about my daughter or my relationship to her. After a few phone calls and running back and forth, we were finally shown our room and allowed to store our belongings there. I was also able to pump. Then Jeramy and I headed to the cafeteria to get something to eat. We knew this surgery was going to take a while, so we needed to do something to distract ourselves. We also met my mom in the cafeteria.

We did not want to wait in the surgery room, so we chose to go upstairs to what they called the Ronald McDonald House. I ate a little bit of food but only felt sick to my stomach. I had my phone glued to my side, waiting for someone to call and update me on how Lillian was doing back in the operating room. I was getting nervous because I still had not heard anything since the surgery started. A few hours later, I got the call to head back down to the PICU. I was told that the surgery went well and that we could see Lillian soon. We were also told that Dr. H would come down shortly to talk to us about how Lillian fared during surgery. We headed down to the PICU waiting room.

Once there, we waited anxiously for her heart surgeon to come through the doors. Dr. H finally walked in and was very straightforward and to the point. He explained how Lillian had done well. He was able to successfully place the Blalock-Taussig (BT) shunt. This is a shunt (a device that allows a small passage for blood flow) that is placed in the heart to increase blood flow in the pulmonary artery. He asked if we had any questions, but we could not think of any. I felt as if I should have questions, but I had no idea what to ask. He stated that they were closing her up and getting ready to take her to her room. It would be about forty-five more minutes before we were allowed to see her.

Those forty-five minutes seemed like hours. I felt a sudden sigh of relief that the surgery was over, but I just wanted to see my baby girl. I needed to see her to know she was okay. I had seen pictures previously of what babies look like after having this procedure, so I was somewhat prepared for what I was about to see. I was ready to face that reality, even though I knew I would feel different because it was my baby that I was going to see hooked up to all of those machines.

My parents were in the waiting room with us. They brought us food to eat while we waited to see Lillian. The talk of blood transfusions came up in our conversations. We soon discovered that Lillian could possibly require a blood transfusion, as many heart babies do after surgery. I had not thought of this prior to surgery, and neither did Jeramy. I said that if Lillian needed blood, I would allow it. Jeramy had a different opinion. He did not want Lillian to receive a blood transfusion because there are risks involved. There is no way to completely test all of the blood, and some things could have been missed during the testing process. He did not want Lillian to be given someone else's blood. This is a conversation that I never thought we would have. I was angry at him. I told him that if Lillian needs blood to keep her alive, then she will get it. I didn't care what he had to say about it. Keeping Lillian alive was more important to me. If she ended up contracting a disease from the blood, then we would deal with that when and if it happened. But until then, he didn't have a say in the matter.

I stormed out of the room—angry! Who the hell did I marry? I couldn't believe this was happening. I was already mad at him in general, and now this? Another reason for me to be completely ticked off. I decided that day that I would be the one to make the call as to whether or not Lillian should get blood, regardless of what Jeramy thought. And by gosh, if she needed it to survive, she was going to get it! When I was ready, I walked back into the PICU waiting room. I wasn't sure if Jeramy was just afraid of a blood transfusion. I believed that if it came down to a life or death situation, he would agree to let Lillian have one. Tensions and emotions were high. I decided to not talk about it again, but I would make the call that she could have a transfusion if she needed it. The PICU nurse finally came out and allowed Jeramy and me to come back and see Lillian. My mom stayed in the waiting room to give us some space.

Chapter 8
That Doesn't Look Like My Baby

We walked to room 2507. This was a double
room, which meant there was a good chance we would
be sharing a room with another child. We were the only
ones in there the first night. Lillian's bed was at the far
side of the room. When I saw her, it broke my heart. She
was lying in a bed with blankets rolled up and placed on
both sides of her. She had an IV pole that had so many
medicines hooked up to it. Her monitor kept going off.
She had a ventilator down her lungs, breathing for her.
She was medically paralyzed and very swollen. Her little
face looked round and wet, her eyes were closed and
swollen, her body was puffy, and I could see bruises on
areas where they had tried to stick her and failed. Her
chest had a big bandage down the middle, in between her
rib cage. A drainage line was coming out of her body
beneath her incision, and there was blood in the line.
This was Lillian, my baby, but she looked nothing like
my baby. The nurses were very sweet and explained to

me about the different medicines she was on and why. They said that the plan was to let Lillian rest tonight. A nurse was stationed in her room the entire time for the first twenty-four hours to make sure she remained stabilized and that they don't miss anything.

My mom was finally able to come back. I could see that it was hard for her to see Lillian like this. It was hard on me as well. Jeramy was pretty quiet and did not say much. The nice thing about this room was that it was big and the couch pulled out into a queen-size bed. Nurses struggled to keep her blood pressures controlled, and they had to keep switching up her Lasix because she would stop peeing and then would pee too much. It was a long night, and I barely got any sleep. But we made it.

The next morning doctors decided to try to wean her off of her paralytics to see if she would wake up some. Jeramy kept bugging me about how he wanted to get out of the hospital for a little while and take me out to lunch. I did not want to leave Lillian. I felt like I was being a bad mom if I left my newborn baby in the hospital. It just didn't feel right. I felt selfish. However, Jeramy was very persistent, and the nurse even started to chime in, agreeing that it was a good idea. I decided to give in and go out to lunch, mainly so Jeramy would shut up and so that maybe he would quit bugging me for a few days about it. Lillian was sedated, so I knew we wouldn't miss anything. It ended up being a pretty nice lunch. We sat outside at a restaurant we had never eaten at before. It felt good to get some fresh air and to eat something other than hospital food. I couldn't help but think I was going to miss something important though, and I was more than ready to get back to the hospital.

The nurse called to let us know that doctors were discussing extubating her. They had decided to remove her from the ventilation. She told us to head back to the hospital so we wouldn't miss it. We paid our tab and rushed back to the hospital. When we arrived in Lillian's room, she was sleeping. She occasionally would wake up crying, and it broke my heart. She looked uncomfortable and scared, and it killed me to see her like that. They ended up deciding that she needed more pain medicines and was too sleepy to extubate. The team met and came to the resolution that it would be best to go ahead and let her rest for the remainder of the day and overnight, and they would try again tomorrow.

That evening we were told we needed to leave our room for an hour or so because there was another heart warrior back in surgery who would have to share a room with us. I tried so hard not to be annoyed, but I couldn't help it. My baby had just had open-heart surgery. You guys put us in this dumb shared room, and now you are telling me that I have to leave my baby. I also did not want to share a room. To be honest, I was annoyed and angry. I felt bad that another heart baby had to have surgery, but I was selfish. I hated leaving Lillian. And the fact that the nurses were telling me I had to leave her side and I didn't have a choice, infuriated me. However, I left because, in the end, I do not like conflict and Lillian was sleeping anyway. We stayed in the PICU waiting room until they told us we could come back in.

When I entered the room, I felt horrible for the little boy who they brought into our room. He looked like he was possibly two. His parents were by his bed, wearing T-Shirts they had made to support him. He was extubated before I went back into the room and looked like he was just resting. The hospital did not furnish a bed for parents on their side of the room. All they had was a chair. I started to feel bad about being so selfish. Any time I had to leave the room to use the restroom, to get a drink, to get something to eat, or to rinse my bottles from pumping, I had to go through their side of the room. I also felt like we needed to be quiet. There were so many things now that I started to stress over.

That night, Jeramy and I pulled out our bed and went to sleep. It was like any other night at the hospital. I looked on my phone and texted some people before I finally drifted off to sleep. I woke up because I heard a noise and sat up in bed. The lights in our room were on, and nurses were surrounding Lillian's bed. A doctor walked over to me and said that Lillian's oxygen and heart rate were dropping, and they are trying to determine the reason why.

I shook Jeramy awake, and he asked me what was happening. I tried to explain it to him, but he didn't understand me. I looked at the clock, and it read 12:57 am. Then I looked at Lillian and saw how blue she looked. "Start CPR. Let's Go!" A nurse started to do compressions on our baby's freshly cut-open chest. I turned and fell into Jeramy's arms as I told him they had started compressions. He quickly jumped up and held onto me. We both hurried out of bed pretty quickly and folded up our bed to allow more space in our now very tight, filled-with-people room. I looked around the room as more and more people started to fill it. Transportation services, two doctors, the fellow, and multiple nurses were in there.

One of the doctors was leading the compressions and trying to figure out Lillian's oxygen levels and heart rate. During this time, all I heard and understood was that our nurse was drawing a pressurized lab by herself. Right when she started to draw the labs, Lillian coded. She was not sure what happened. The doctor who was in charge was asking so many questions to these people. He was asking nurses to take turns doing compressions on Lillian. Everything seemed like it was a movie. It was as if everything was going in slow motion, and I was just watching from afar. But it wasn't a movie; it was real life. Everything was happening so quickly, and I was right there witnessing it all. I was a mess. I couldn't stop crying. At one point, Jeramy called my parents and his to let them know what was happening. I was not ready to say goodbye to my baby.In my mind I was planning a funeral and wondering how I was going to leave this hospital empty handed.

As I watched I was begging God to please let Lillian live. I was crumbling inside. My baby was not breathing. Her small and fragile body was limp. She was blue. I watched nurses take turns doing compressions. They were pushing on her chest as they counted the compressions. 1... 2... 3... By the time one nurse got to 30 a few times, she would switch with another nurse, and then another would start after her, and then back to the first nurse again. I felt like I was dying. I looked at Jeramy and told him that I felt as if I was going to pass out. He told me I better pull it together. They needed to focus on Lillian and not me passing out on the floor, so I did my best to pull myself together. After all, I was a heart mom. I had to be strong. They say God only gives you as much as you can handle. I knew that was a lie though, because I couldn't handle this. The first round of compressions lasted approximately five minutes. Lillian came back and her oxygen saturations and heart rate were stabilized. Within a few moments though, she coded again. This time she wasn't coming back as quickly. I could see fear and confusion on everyone's faces.

Then, in came the hospital's chaplain. She introduced herself to me and asked if she could pray with us. All I wanted to do was kick her out of the room. I wasn't saying goodbye to my baby. This wasn't happening to me. I felt like I was going to pass out. When the hospital staff asked the chaplain to come in, I knew it was bad. I knew that they were preparing me for the worst. But instead of kicking her out, I agreed to let her stay and pray. I begged and pleaded with God in that moment to not make me an angel mommy. I hadn't wanted to be a heart mom in the first place. I definitely didn't want to be an angel mom. I knew I wasn't strong enough for that. From the other side of the curtain, I could hear the mom of the boy we were sharing a room with crying. I knew they were awake, and they could hear the commotion from our room.

Luckily, Lillian was still intubated. It turns out that they were able to keep her breathing with the help of a machine. Dr. H and the red team came in, but they could not figure out what had happened. Lillian stabilized and they continued to let her rest. They had an echocardiogram (ECHO) and an electrocardiogram (EKG), a device that measures the electrical activity of the heart over a period of time, performed on her, all of which looked fine.

They also ended up giving her a blood transfusion. It was strange that we had just argued about this two days prior. Dr. H let us know that they were going to give Lillian blood. I looked at Jeramy, who was silent. I said that it was fine and gave my consent for them to give her blood. We received no explanation as to why this had happened. I wanted answers but was happy enough knowing that Lillian was strong enough and had survived. Lillian was a fighter, and she was going to continue to fight. Her time with us was not over yet!

Once Lillian was stable, the dad of the boy we were sharing a room with talked to Jeramy. I am not sure what all they said, but I know they talked about what had just happened and how they were praying for us. He said that our situation brought back a lot of memories for them. They talked about how strong these heart babies are and how much they go through. He was a very nice guy, and I am happy he reached out and talked to my husband. It was good to know we weren't alone. Thankfully for this family, their stay in the PICU was short lived, and they were able to be transferred to the Transitional Care Unit (TCU), a step-down unit and the last unit a family visits before going home the next day.

Today, June 7, was my brother's birthday. My parents, he, and his fiancé all came up to the hospital to comfort me. My mom was crying. She is my angel mom. She had been pregnant with identical twin girls early in her marriage and had lost one of them to heart failure twenty-four hours after birth. I know this time in her life was traumatic, and seeing Lillian the way she was and hearing that she had almost died I know set her off. She was terrified for me. She didn't want me to live that heartache. Not to mention, it brought back a ton of memories for her.

We had a lot of visitors today, and many

unanswered questions, but there were lots of relieved faces to see how strong Lillian is, and we were all just thankful that she was still alive. I was emotionally drained. No one ever tells a mother that things like this can happen. I thought Lillian would have heart surgery, recovery time, and then go home until she was big enough for the next surgery to repair her heart. I thought I knew how hard it was to be a heart mom, but in reality, I was just learning. Lillian was going to really challenge me over the next few months of her life. I thought I was already at rock bottom, but boy, was I in for a treat.

The next day Lillian was extubated and things seemed to finally be going smoothly. She was allowed to drink clear Pedialyte to see how she could handle eating. She did not seem to like it very much, so it was decided to let her drink some breast milk. She ate okay, considering it her first time ever eating. She was not eating enough though, so the decision was made to place a nasogastric feeding tube (NG tube) in her nose so that whatever she did not eat by mouth, would be put in her stomach until she was strong enough to eat the entire bottle on her own. It felt so good to see Lillian make small improvements. The fact that she was able to finally eat breastmilk that I had been pumping like crazy for her, filled me with joy.

The next day Lillian's drainage line was pulled. I watched the nurses do this, and it made me nauseous. I wanted to be involved in everything they did with her. I didn't want to miss a thing, and I wanted them to inform me of every little and big thing they did. The doctor pulled her line and blood filled her stomach. Nurses applied a lot of pressure to her stomach until the bleeding stopped. Then they cleaned the area and placed a bandage over it. I learned how to perform dressing changes, and I watched as Lillian was given her first sponge bath.

Once her main lines were pulled, I was finally able to hold Lillian again. This time, however, I was allowed to get her out of bed myself. I was very nervous when doing this, but I wanted to hold her all day long, so I had to overcome my fear of accidentally hurting her. I had to be very careful when picking her up because her incision and chest were still healing. We would not be allowed to pick her up by her underarms for six weeks post-op due to the healing process and the fact that it could cause a lot of pain to Lillian. We had to scoop her up by placing our hands underneath her head and bottom. I was also allowed to feed her and to change her when she peed and pooped. As the days went on, I was finally starting to feel like her mom. It was an exhilarating feeling, and things really started to look up for us. I also grew less nervous to move her out of her bed and put her back into bed.

It was time to share a room again. I was feeling very discouraged at this point. This was now the second time I was being asked to leave Lillian's side so that another heart patient could share a room with us. This time it was a girl. She was beautiful and had gorgeous curly hair. I kept thinking about how hard this must be for these families. It's difficult to see Lillian like this, but I can't imagine what it must be like to have a baby, who in all actuality is no longer a baby anymore, still getting these surgeries. Again, the child's family was in the room and were all wearing shirts to support their daughter. I wanted to get shirts like those made for Lillian. I could easily tell this was not their first rodeo, as far as heart surgeries were concerned. They seemed very knowledgeable and content.

Jeramy's parents came into town to visit Lillian. I was happy to see them, but I was in a very dark place. Jeramy kept trying to get me to leave the hospital again, but I didn't want to desert Lillian. I was struggling with trying to decide what to do. I knew my husband wanted to spend time with me, but I also knew I didn't want to leave Lillian alone. His parents asked if we would go out to eat with them. They had traveled all the way from Kentucky to spend the weekend with us. I decided to go out to eat and told Jeramy that it needed to be a quick lunch. I wanted to eat and go straight back to the hospital.

We arrived at Hard Rock Café. It was a much needed lunch, but I couldn't focus. My mind was still at the hospital with Lillian. I choked down my burger as fast as possible in hopes that we would quickly head back to the hospital. I had not planned to be gone long, so I didn't bring my breast pump with me. My breasts were full, and I was due to pump. I thought we were heading straight back to the hospital, but Jeramy's stepdad stopped at the hotel. They had brought their dog with them and needed to take him out. I understood that the dog needed to do his business, but I was hurt inside. I wanted to be back at the hospital. Nothing else in the world mattered to me.

Jeramy's stepdad decided to take the dog for a walk. When he returned, which felt like forever and a day, he gave the dog a treat and then started to eat cookies and hang out. At this point, Jeramy knew I was growing inpatient, but he didn't say anything. Again, it was a tough situation I found myself in. I still felt like no one understood.

His folks even mentioned how they wish they had known the hotel has a pool because we all could have swam and stayed the night there if we wanted. I didn't understand why they had even come, knowing that Lillian is in the hospital and expecting me to want to hang out and leave my newborn baby alone. I was crushed inside. I knew that living in the hospital was not fun. I'm sure they were bored at the hospital, but that's where I wanted to be. Don't get me wrong, I love spending time with my in-laws, but now was not the time. I needed to be with my baby, not out and about having a "good" time. I knew they were just trying to help us out, and they probably thought I needed a break. Of course, staying in a hotel is always nicer than staying in a hospital, but I didn't want that. My baby was in the hospital, not in the hotel. I didn't care about comfort or mental breaks.I again felt the harsh reality that no one really understood what I was going through.

They had never lived with the harsh reality of having a heart baby, but this was my life now. I couldn't expect them to fully understand, but I was feeling sadder and more alone than ever. Jeramy grew up with cystic fibrosis, so I knew that they understood what it is like to have a chronically ill child, but it was still different. They finally dropped us back off at the hospital, and they went back to the hotel for the night. I was so happy though, because they took a load of our clothes back to the hotel with them to wash for us. I needed some fresh clothes.

We had some problems in our PICU room with our sink that night. This is when we really started to get to know the family with whom we were sharing a room. Not to mention both of our daughters had different nurses, and both of our monitors kept sounding an alarm because medicines were depleted or needed to be switched out, but no nurse was ever in sight. We laughed as the day continued on like this, trying to not become annoyed and realizing that things could be worse. We ended up naming the other girl's dad, *The Voice of Room 2507* because he ventured out into the hallways multiple times to find nurses to silence our machines. Hearing a constant beep for hours on end grew very tiring and annoying.

When Preslee would come up to the hospital to visit, she and the other little girl started to play together. The day that this girl got to go to the TCU, Preslee was there. It was her birthday. My sweet baby girl was now two years old, and we were spending it at the hospital. The little girl was wearing Minnie Mouse pajamas and had the same Minnie Mouse stuffed animal and baby doll as Preslee. The girls were very close in age as well.

The little girl walked into our room and started to play with Preslee. She gave Preslee one of her Minnie Mouse balloons in honor of Preslee's birthday. The girls shared Preslee's magnetic dress-up characters. Her grandmas were both there the entire time as well and are the sweetest ladies ever. I am so thankful to have met this family.

Finally, I was meeting more heart moms. More people who could relate to what I was going through. Maybe sharing a room with another family wasn't so bad after all. I felt sad though. I felt like Lillian was stuck and not progressing now. Again, we are in a room alone. I felt bad that Preslee had to spend her birthday at a hospital. Jeramy and I decided to take her to a restaurant to get something to eat and to spend a little one-on-one time with her. My awesome mom stayed at the hospital with Lillian. Two heart patients had come and gone now, but here we are still stuck in this room going nowhere fast. The room was empty again, and I started to feel hopeless.

The rest of this stay, our biggest struggles with Lillian were getting her to eat and weaning her off of oxygen. A speech therapist came in a few times a day to teach me how to feed my baby. It was so weird learning how to feed a baby. This is something I thought babies just naturally knew how to do, but it turns out that they forget how to do this when they are not allowed to eat for the first week of their life. The days seemed to be going slower than ever. And again, we were asked to leave our room so that another heart baby could come into the room. This time, it was a newborn baby boy. He was so tiny. The mom came into the room and sat in a chair. She cried while looking over him. I could relate to how she was feeling. My heart broke for her. The next day, I was alone in Lillian's room. I heard this mother crying again, and I felt I needed to console her. I asked her if this was her first baby. She told me yes, and then broke down.

I could tell she needed to vent, so I just listened. She told me that she had delivered her baby at home. Everything was perfect at first. But a couple days later, her baby turned blue and had to be flight lifted to the hospital late at night. Our room was right next to the landing pad. I remembered having heard the helicopter land. I couldn't help but wonder if it had been them on that flight. Her baby had to have immediate surgery performed on him. I felt awful for that mom because she was heartbroken and going through a lot of the same emotions I was going through. I could imagine how she felt, thinking everything was fine and then seeing her baby that way. That's how I felt when I found out about Lillian's condition. My heart broke for her. I gave her my number and told her how sorry I was for her and her baby. I let her know that I understood how hard this was for her, and if she ever needed someone to vent to, she was welcome to call or text me. I expressed how we heart mamas are all in this together and said I would pray for her. She never reached out, but that's okay. I pray that her venting to me helped her in some way. That same day, Lillian moved to the TCU. I was so excited because it was a day for which I had been longing. It was a breakthrough for Lillian. She was finally making progress.

Our first nurse's name was Jane. She was so sweet, and she and Lillian shared the same birthday. Jane became Lillian's "birthday buddy." This was what she called Lillian, and it set my heart at ease. It was so nice to have a caring nurse who helped make light of the situation. Being in the TCU, however, was nothing like being in the PICU. The nurses are more nonexistent. This made me even more terrified to leave Lillian. The rooms in TCU were not as nice. There was only a small chair that folds out into a very small bed. The beds for babies weren't even as nice. Lillian looked like she was in a cage. Her bed had metal rails all the way around it. They were very old beds, and the sides were very hard to lift and lower to get to her. Everything was outdated compared to the PICU. The only bonus was having a bathroom in the room, but we had to share it with the neighboring room. It definitely was not homey, but I tried not to care. This was Lillian's last step before we would get to bring her home. I was terrified by not having a nurse there constantly. It was a harsh reality. Not being able to look out of our room and see a group of doctors staring at my baby's monitor on a wall full of screens brought fear to me. What if something happened to Lillian? Is anyone even going to know? This made me even more ready to take Lillian home.

As the days passed, Lillian grew a little stronger. Her incision was healing nicely, and she was slowly starting to eat better. I had to feed her less and less milk through her NG tube because she was eating more by mouth. The speech therapist was still coming by and working with her. Jeramy was no longer staying in the hospital with me, as he had to return to work. I spent most days alone. I was bored, sad, and lonely. I was cooped up in a room where I couldn't see the outside world. It felt as though I was a prisoner in a hospital. Lillian was not allowed to breastfeed because nurses needed to track how much she was eating. Plus, I was told it put too much strain on her heart. We were still

getting daily visits from the "Red Team" (cardiac team).
Her heart surgeon visited her daily and listened to her
heart. Other than that, nothing changed. This was the life
I was living. This is what it is like to be a heart mom. I
tried to be okay with it, and I tried to accept it. More
than anything, I was so thankful that Lillian was alive
and striving … slowly.

The only conversations Jeramy and I had were when he
would call and ask how Lillian was. He would tell me
how Preslee was doing, but other than that, we were
distant. I was pushing him away as I had an anger built
up. I was handling Lillian's situation my way, and he
was handling it in his own way. I didn't try to understand
his way. Instead, I had a fire build up in me- an anger. I
became more and more distant. I had too much on my
plate to worry about his feelings. I didn't care to
understand. It was a terrible feeling, but it was what it
was.

Chapter 9
Ready to Go Home

    Certain protocols had to be followed in order for us to bring Lillian home. Jeramy and I had to take a mandatory CPR class because she was a NICU baby and a heart baby. We invited my Maw-Maw to come with us. She was the one who would watch both of my girls when I returned to work. The thought of having to leave Lillian made me nervous, but I also knew I still had a couple of months to talk myself into being okay with it. As a teacher, I am fortunate to be off work during the summer. I was ready to finally go home and try to enjoy what was left of the summer. I couldn't even tell you if it was cold or hot out. I didn't know when it was sunny, rainy, or cloudy. The only weather I was ever aware of was the temperature in the TCU room. It was always freezing. Here I was, wearing hoodies and sweatpants every day in the summer. It's a weird metaphor for how I was feeling throughout our entire stay at the hospital.

During CPR training, we were taught how to perform compressions on a newborn baby. This brought back memories of the morning when Lillian had coded twice. My stomach was in knots. At one point, I left to "use the restroom." I actually did need to go, because my stomach was killing me, but I also knew it would bring great relief for me to escape from that room. I hid in the stall for about five minutes while I cried my eyes out. The wounds were too fresh. I was not yet healed from seeing my blue lifeless baby. When we had to practice CPR on the little manikin baby, it killed me. All I could envision was Lillian's blue body. Again, I didn't want to cry in front of anyone. I displayed a fake strength to others because I was afraid to let anyone see me fall. I needed to be Lillian's voice. I am her mother. I am supposed to be strong, brave, and fearless. I pulled myself together, wiped the tears from my face, and walked back in the room.

We continued with CPR training and hoped we would never be called on to use it. I now had to rely on my Maw-Maw, my husband, and myself to keep Lillian alive, should she go into cardiac arrest again. I prayed that I would remember everything I had learned and would be able to put it into practice if that moment ever came. This was not the first time I had been trained in CPR, but it was the first time that I had to complete training for the sake of my baby. The what ifs came flooding back, and I questioned myself more now than ever. What if Lillian went into cardiac arrest and I froze up and couldn't save her? What if I failed my baby and now her death was my fault? I knew I shouldn't think like this; it was insane. I had to stop these crazy thoughts from running through my mind. I would deal with these imaginary scenarios if, or when, they ever happen. I offered up a prayer to God: Heavenly Father, you have gifted me with the most beautiful and precious baby in the world. I'm placing her back in your loving hands for safekeeping. Please don't let anything happen to Lillian!

Our daughter was required to have a car seat test. This is a test in which a baby must sit in a car seat for ninety minutes without oxygen levels dropping. If the baby fails the test, it cannot go home yet. This got me thinking again. Our ride home from the hospital is over an hour, and I will be the one driving. Lillian won't be hooked up to any monitors. What if her oxygen levels do drop? How will I know? I can't see her when I am driving. I can't look at her chest to make sure she is breathing, and I can't touch her little body to feel if it is still warm. Anxiety and fear were filling my body. Thankfully, Lillian passed with flying colors. She fell asleep in the car seat and even stayed in it longer than ninety minutes because I didn't want to wake her. We were now another step closer to going home. She still needed an ECHO, EKG, X-Ray, and to lose the NG tube. The only reason we still remained in the hospital was because Lillian was not eating well.

Doctors discussed sending her home with an NG tube. I was comfortable with it, so they trained me on how to place it correctly and how to recognize if it is in her stomach by using a stethoscope. I was happy to be given this task. Not only did it make me feel important, but it also was one less thing I had to rely on nurses to do for Lillian. I was now in charge of the feedings. I was campaigning more than ever for Lillian to be able to eat by mouth. I didn't want her to have to go home with an NG tube, and doctors didn't want her to either. I felt like I was becoming a nurse because I knew so much more about medical issues now than I ever imagined possible.

I learned more about her diagnosis. I knew how to read a monitor and how to read rhythms on the monitor to determine whether or not it was giving an accurate reading. I learned how to listen to Lillian's heart and how to perform CPR. I was comfortable picking her up without lifting her by her underarms. I could now hold her, change the dressings on her wounds, feed her, and use an NG tube. I had developed an affection for the Red Team and became very close to a lot of gifted nurses. Despite all my newly learned skills and my readiness to go home, I still didn't trust myself. I doubted that I alone would be enough to care for Lillian. I was terrified that something bad would happen, and that I would not be able to save her on my own.

During one of Lillian's dressing changes, I noticed a very small white dot on her incision. One of the cardiac nurses came upstairs, and she rubbed me the wrong way. She made me feel stupid. I mentioned to her that I didn't know if the dot I was seeing was a puss pocket—she interrupted me with a "no" before I could even finish getting the rest of the words out. The lady was very rude and said no with a snarky chuckle. She said there is no way that tiny little dot could possibly be a puss pocket, that it was probably just glue leftover from the surgery. I was trying to be Lillian's voice, but I felt so dumb in that moment. The nurse's attitude suggested that she knew everything about all things. I did not care for her one bit. I believed something was wrong with that small dot. Because she was the professional, I figured she knew more about it than I did. I let it go and continued to monitor it, as the nurse had said.

During this hospital stay, I was nicknamed "the mother who milks like a cow." I thought it was hilarious. I was filling the freezers with my breastmilk, and they had to store some of it in the NICU. I was proudly producing around sixty ounces a day, because I would fill two eight-ounce bottles with each pump. This helped pass the time and also made me feel like I could do something for Lillian on my own. This nickname would follow me through the rest of Lillian's hospital stays. I was determined to keep producing milk for my daughter even though she could not breastfeed. She was not gaining much weight, so formula had to be added to each bottle of breastmilk. This is referred to as "fortifying to add calories." Because it was beneficial to Lillian, I did it, even though it seemed strange to me that "the mother who milks like a cow" also has to buy formula. Being a heart mom was alien to me, but I went with it. I was willing to do whatever I had to do for Lillian.

Finally, on June 17, a day after mine and Jeramy's five-year wedding anniversary, Lillian had an ECHO and EKG. Both looked great. She achieved her goal for the amount of food she was required to eat for her last two feedings, so the NG tube was pulled out. We were finally being discharged! I was ecstatic but terrified. I loaded all of our things into the car and then placed Lillian in her car seat. This would be her first car ride. We said goodbye to some of our favorite nurses and headed out. When I walked outside, it was hot and sunny. This was the first time Lillian had been outside the hospital. She got her first glimpse of that beautiful, shining sun. For the very first time, she could feel a soft breeze blowing on her and breathe in some fresh air. She had finally been freed from all the monitors and machines and was on her way home.

On our way there, I picked up Preslee from my parents' house. It felt so foreign to have both of my babies in the car with me. I felt a sense of freedom, and for the first time in a long time, I was happy and at peace. The darkness was turning to light. At home, Lillian still had to take medicine. She was on baby aspirin, which would act as a blood thinner; Poly-Vi-Sol to give her iron; Lasix to help remove water weight from her body; and Pepcid to help with stomach acid and gas. I still had to change dressings on her incisions twice a day, but doing so made me feel like a terrible mother because she would cry every single time. She hated it, and therefore I hated it too.

Being home was very peaceful for me. I was so thankful to have both of my daughters under the same roof in their own home where they belonged. I had to give Lillian sponge baths, and although Preslee did get a little jealous, she loved to help with them. When I swaddled Lillian, I had to swaddle Preslee. When I kissed Lillian, I had to kiss Preslee. When I held Lillian, I had to hold Preslee. When Lillian was not in her bouncy seat, Preslee was in it. She was my little helper and wanted to be a part of everything I did with Lillian, including the times I changed Lillian's wound dressings. She would rub Lillian's head and shush her while she cried, telling her it was okay. She would say, "Awe, poor sissy. Sissy has boo-boos. I want boo-boos too." I would smile at Preslee and tell her that mommy doesn't want her to have boo-boos. It broke my heart to hear her say she wanted them too. I reassured her that Lillian was brave and strong and that her boo-boos would turn into lovely beauty scars soon.

Lillian still was not eating as well as she should. With every dressing change, I would look at the spot on her incision and watch it grow larger. I still instinctively knew it did not look right, but I did everything I could to keep it clean. It was hard for me to change her bandages. She would cry every time I peeled the long bandage off her chest, but it ran further down her body than the incision, so I couldn't do it quickly. She hated when I put Betadine on the wound. I don't think she was a fan of the coldness the Betadine caused. She would scream the entire time. It broke my heart because I hated to see her in pain but couldn't take it away for her. I wished that I could trade places with her, that I could give her my heart, so she would never have to endure this pain again. I would do it in a heartbeat. I don't know how many times I tried to hold back the tears as I gently peeled the bandages off Lillian's chest. I would whisper to her in a very shaky voice, telling her how brave and strong she is, but the alligator tears slowly crept out of my eyes and rolled down my cheeks. I didn't want her to see me crying. I had to be strong and brave like her. But it was so hard.

I was enjoying my role as a mommy of two. However, it was taking its toll on me. Luckily, Lillian was a sound sleeper, so having to constantly wake up in the middle of the night was not on our menu. Even so, it was hard work pumping every two hours, feeding Lillian, cooking breakfast, lunch, and dinner each day, and trying to potty train Preslee, who said she didn't want to use the potty because she wanted to be a baby too. Between giving sponge baths, giving Preslee baths, and trying to shower myself, I was exhausted. And on top of that, I struggled with sleeping comfortably. I would find myself waking up constantly to check on Lillian and touch her chest to make sure she was still breathing. I was also having nightmares. I would wake up multiple times during the night, sweating and terrified. I had dreams in which Lillian went into cardiac arrest, and I couldn't save her. I dreamt that a helicopter had to land in our subdivision to pick her up because we lived too far from the hospital. I was a wreck.

We were sent home with pulse-ox and oxygen machines to use just in case they were needed. We were trained on how to use both, but the only one we ever used was the pulse-ox. Nurses had instructed us to only hook Lillian up to it for spot checks. But that wasn't going to happen. I remember seeing my baby lifeless and blue at one in the morning. There was no way on Earth I would be able to sleep without knowing Lillian was constantly hooked up to the monitor. Each night before bedtime, I would hook her up and have her sleep with it on. Anytime it would sound an alarm, I would jump out of bed and check on her. Her heart would still brady every once in a while, but other than that, her oxygen levels were good, even though they have always been a little higher since her surgery. Dr. H was not happy that they were so high, because typically he wants a heart baby with a BT shunt to stay in the 75-85 range. Lillian, however, had registered in the 90s since her surgery.

Chapter 10
Trust a Mother's Intuition

Life was going well the first few days after we got home. Lillian was required to have weight checks twice a week. Heart babies are generally on the smaller side, and because she was not eating well, her doctor wanted to make sure she was gaining weight. We were assigned an in-home nurse named Harleigh, a very sweet country lady. I thought her visits were pointless because all she would do is come in and place Lillian on a scale, record her weight, and then leave. If anything, her visits became more of an inconvenience because she would never notify me when she was coming until she was already in town and practically at my door. All I knew for certain was that she would be here every Tuesday and Friday.

There were a lot of activities to keep me busy: giving Lillian daily medications at all different times, feedings every three hours (and I had to really coax her to eat), pumping every three hours, in-home nurse visits, pediatric appointments for shots, follow-up appointments with the heart surgeon, and cardiology appointments. I wanted to feel happy to be home, but we were so busy with appointments that I felt as though I really wasn't getting a break from this new reality. We were constantly on the go. I felt terrible for Preslee because I thought she was not enjoying her summer. She didn't ask for this; none of us did. But this was our life now, and it is what it is. At each appointment I made sure to show everyone Lillian's spot on her incision because it kept looking worse. Each person would agree that it looked abnormal but always shrugged it off as possibly nothing other than a stitch popping or suggested that it was "just healing."

Lillian's newborn screening came back. Her pediatrician called me one night at 5 pm. I thought that was a strange time to call, as the office was closed, but I answered the phone just the same. She informed me that Lillian's screening flagged cystic fibrosis. I explained how that couldn't be possible because I had the genetic screening test performed before we even went through IVF. She explained to me that genetic screening is not one hundred percent accurate because it is impossible to test for all of the genetic mutations that go along with cystic fibrosis. Lillian flagged for the same rare mutation that her daddy has, G551D. I couldn't believe what I was hearing. As if having CHD wasn't bad enough, now she might have cystic fibrosis as well? I was crushed. Jeramy was very concerned and was afraid to even touch her.

I understood why he didn't want to hold her, as CF patients can pass lung infections to each other very easily. But this angered me inside. I was exhausted, and I needed help. I was more alone now than ever before. Everything was being piled on my plate, and my responsibilities were increasing tenfold. I felt like a single mother. He had been afraid he might pass his infections to Lillian, and once someone with cystic fibrosis gets lung infections, they never go away. He didn't want to feel responsible for something so serious. But he is Lillian's dad. If she has CF, then it is what it is. What are we going to do? Is he going to avoid her for the rest of his life? Again, the walls were caving in. I was suffocating and falling into a deeper depression. I was heartbroken knowing Jeramy wouldn't hold her. He wouldn't come anywhere near her. Although I understood the reasoning behind his decision, I was still angry, and I took it out on him. I pushed him further away again. Life was so unfair.

I watched Lillian like a hawk. One day we stood outside in the sun, and Lillian started sweating on my black T-shirt. One of the signs of CF is salty skin. When I held her away from me, there were salt crystals on my T-shirt. I couldn't believe it. I told her cardiologist, Dr. G, and he couldn't believe it either. He said it would certainly not be good for Lillian if she did have CF because it would greatly complicate things with her heart. She already wasn't getting enough blood flow to her lungs. She definitely wasn't healthy, so it would be very, very bad if she has CF.

Our pediatrician requested that a sweat test be completed. We went to the hospital and sat in a small room. They cleaned Lillian's arms and stuck small round Band-Aid-looking things on her skin to collect sweat. Then they wrapped heating pads around her arms and bundled her up. We needed her to sweat. After an hour, they were not able to obtain enough sweat from her because she was too small and also a newborn; therefore, she couldn't produce enough sweat. We would have to wait until she was bigger to perform the test again—at least another month. This was heartbreaking. It meant I was going to have to watch my husband avoid his daughter for another month, which meant all responsibility for her care was going to fall on me. I tried to understand. I could kind of see where he was coming from and did understand to a degree, so I hid my feelings and sucked it up. But I was more terrified now than ever. I hated having to face the unknown and the uncertainty of what was going to happen next.

After her sweat test, I took Lillian by the heart center where her surgeon worked. The hospital was over an hour from my home, so I wanted someone to look at the spot on her incision while we were already there. The nurse looked at it and shrugged it off. She said it didn't look that bad and to just keep it cleaned and covered. I have watched this spot grow for some time now, and I've seen that it keeps getting worse, but everyone else looks at it and acts as if it's no big deal. They are the experts, so I decided to trust them and went on my way.

I took Lillian to her cardiologist a week later for her appointment. Dr. G took one look at her incision and said he did not like the look of it. He called her heart surgeon and explained that he didn't think it looked good. I was directed to head straight to the hospital to let him examine her. I was happy that someone had finally listened to me and recognized my mother's intuition. I thought that for once someone is taking me seriously! I wasn't surprised that person was Dr. G. He never lets me down.

I took Lillian to the hospital and undressed her down to her diaper, like always. Dr. H came in and said that her incision didn't look bad, but it did look like it could be infected. He took a needle and cut open the bottom part of the incision with it. Lillian was screaming. I could not believe he was doing this to her. He took a swab, placed it into the incision, and swirled it around. He explained that he would send it to the lab to be cultured and would then go ahead and admit Lillian to the hospital. He wanted to start her on IV antibiotics just in case her lab cultures showed bacteria growing on them.

We were sent to the TCU, where they placed an IV in Lillian. She has always been a hard one to stick, so it hurt me to watch them try three times to place an IV and fail each time. On the fourth try, transportation services came and placed her IV on the first try. I was grateful that they had come into the room. The nurse who placed Lillian's IV was singing to her and rubbing her head. Finally, someone was showing compassion to her. It helped calm her a little, but I could tell she was exhausted from crying.

She was started on an IV medication to clear up her infections. It was now July, a month after I had first noticed this spot. I was happy that they were finally taking care of it, but I was also angry that it had taken a whole month for someone to trust my intuition and do something about it. I proudly made sure to point it out at every single appointment. We stayed in the hospital for three days this time. The culture that her surgeon took never grew bacteria on it. The Red Team stopped by and asked why we were back in the hospital so soon. They are my peace and comfort when I am in the hospital with Lillian. I trust them immensely and love that we always see the same group of employees regardless of why we are there. I know her heart is being watched closely.

I felt trapped in life. All of my immediate family members were going to my parents' lake house for a Fourth of July celebration. Jeramy, Preslee, Lillian, and I were all supposed to go. But now Lillian was in the hospital again. I was disappointed that Preslee would miss out on the fun again, so I asked Jeramy if he would go ahead and take Preslee to my parents' lake house. I felt like I was stuck between a rock and a hard place. I was conflicted between being jealous that I didn't get to go have fun while Jeramy did and knowing there was no way I would leave Lillian in the hospital. The dilemma was easily solved because I felt it was unfair that Lillian couldn't go too. I pushed my feelings deeper inside again and dealt with it. I was becoming very good at this, or so I thought.

After three days, Lillian was able to go home. She was given a month's prescription of oral antibiotics. I made sure to give it to her daily as instructed. We were home just in time to celebrate the Fourth of July with Jeramy and Preslee. Our neighborhood always hosts a fireworks display, so we took the girls to watch. A few of my family members and friends came over and celebrated with us. We had a small party at the house, and people came over and swam for a little bit. I had to beg Jeramy to get in the pool with Preslee because Lillian couldn't be outside in the heat, let alone get in the pool, and I didn't like the thought of her being outside without me. I was not allowed to get in the pool yet; women must wait six weeks after delivery to swim in a chlorine pool or to soak in any type of water for that matter. So I stayed inside, like I always do, feeling depressed again simply because I did not want to leave

Lillian's side and have fun without her.

The next couple of weeks seemed pretty normal, (whatever normal even means anymore). I was trying to adjust to being the mom of two beautiful girls. Luckily, I was off work for the summer. I tried to enjoy my time off while Jeramy worked. I even managed to work a couple of times on getting my classroom ready for the new school year, which was quickly approaching. One day I took the girls to work with me, and another first grade teacher who I work with picked up Lillian and was loving on her. Preslee was proud to show off her baby sister. The teacher walked out of my classroom with Lillian to show my baby to her husband, and Preslee chased after her. She stomped her little foot and said, "That's my baby. Put my baby back in there," as she pointed to my classroom. We lost it; we were laughing so hard. But in that very moment I realized how close and special the bond was that these two girls shared. Preslee truly loves Lillian and will always protect her. I needed that reassurance.

Open house snuck up on me, and I had to leave the girls to meet all of my new students. I was so excited to see twenty-one energetic first graders smiling at me. I tried to remember all of their names. I was thrilled to be teaching again but wasn't ready for the summer to be over. I felt like I had lived in a hospital all summer long. I wasn't ready to go back to work just yet. Some of my former students came into my class and gave me hugs, which reassured me that I had done the right thing by returning to work. Not that I had much of a choice in the matter. I honestly couldn't afford not to work. The two-hour open house ended quickly, and I rushed to get the girls. I could not wait to finally be able to see Lillian again. I had never left her before, and I hated that I couldn't be there to save her if she needed me.

Sunday rolled around, and Lillian was not acting like herself. She was fussy and tired. Her oxygen levels were now in the 70s, occasionally dropping into the 60s. We checked her levels on multiple extremities just in case we were not getting accurate results. We also switched out the pulse oximeter cords to see if maybe something was wrong with them. But we were still getting the same readings. Two small puss pockets appeared on Lillian's incision in the exact spot where she had developed that weird white spot that I kept pointing out to people. Fear filled my body. I knew something was not right. We packed our bags and headed to the emergency room.

Chapter 11
This Wasn't Supposed to Happen

When we arrived at the emergency room, we immediately let them know that Lillian is a heart baby. Because of this, we were quickly ushered to an examination room. ER attendants connected her to a pulse ox right away, and her stats were all over the place. Her numbers were staying in the upper 70s, and they were okay with that. I kept reminding them that Lillian's levels normally show in the 90s range. This wasn't normal for her. They kept telling me that as babies continue to grow, their oxygen levels lower because the BT shunt does not grow with them. I am by no means stupid. I had already conducted extensive research, and I knew this. But I also can rely on my motherly intuition, and I was positive this was not right. Someone from the cardiology team came in and looked at the spots on Lillian's chest. They were taking pictures of them and vacillating between whether they should act fast and do something about it or just monitor it. Unfortunately for Lillian, both heart surgeons had already left the hospital.

Dr. H needed to get to the airport, so the hospital's other heart surgeon had volunteered to take him. The nurse took pictures of Lillian's incision and sent them to the other heart surgeon. He looked at them and told her to admit Lillian to the hospital and he would view them in greater depth when he returned. They assigned us to a room in the TCU and placed Lillian on oxygen. My baby girl was so sleepy. I could tell something was not right. I hoped for the best but feared for the worst.

The heart surgeon came in and examined the two puss pockets. He said that something definitely did not look right, but he would wait until morning to reexamine them to see if there were any changes. The next morning rolled around, and he looked at them again. He said that for the time being he was not going to do anything because they looked better than they had the night before. By happenstance the surgeon's assistant, Debbie, was present and decided to further investigate Lillian's puss pockets. She was familiar with Lillian and knew she frequently "misbehaved." This was a joke among all of us, including the doctors in the PICU, which started the night/morning when Lillian had coded. "Misbehaved" was code for Lillian does her own thing and doesn't follow the rules regarding what is *supposed* to happen. Debbie decided it would be beneficial to go ahead and

117

perform a CT scan. Later that day Lillian was wheeled downstairs to complete the test and was brought back to her room an hour later. We waited for a little while to find out the results.

The heart surgeon came in and sat down in a chair, which is never a good sign. I had butterflies in my stomach and tears were starting to form. He explained to me that Lillian's infection was growing dangerously toward her heart and that he would have to operate. He apologized that Dr. H was not available to perform the surgery but promised me that he would clean out the infection and take excellent care of Lillian. He said he was surprised by how well Lillian was acting in light of how sick she was and taking into consideration all of her health concerns. I was relieved that I had noticed and kept an eye on these puss pockets and brought her in when I did, because multiple things could have gone wrong very quickly. If we would have waited another day or so, my baby would have become very ill.

Lillian was supposed to have her second sweat test completed to determine whether or not she had cystic fibrosis. I asked the nurses to please complete the test while she was an inpatient because I was anxious to know if she had CF. They agreed to perform the test the next morning. They again cleaned both arms and placed the round sticker gadgets to her arms to catch sweat. Then they swaddled her arms with the purple heating pads.

I held Lillian and loved on her for the entire hour. I made sure to hold her tight so that I could transfer some of my body heat to her. I did not want to be told yet again that she didn't produce enough sweat. I thoroughly enjoyed this hour with her, as it wasn't often that I could play a role in her care. This was one time when I was able to actually participate and feel as though I had helped in some small way. I sang her favorite song, "You are my Sunshine," to her, played with her, talked to her, and kept her as close to my body as possible. When the hour was up, she had actually produced enough sweat! I was elated that we would finally get results. Her sweat was sent down to the lab, and within a few hours, the results were back. Lillian's salt levels on both arms were eleven, which meant that she did not have cystic fibrosis. I was in disbelief and was so happy that I cried happy tears and called Jeramy to give him the good news. A huge weight had been lifted off our shoulders, as this was obviously the best possible outcome for Lillian.

The next morning at 9 am, we walked alongside the nurses as they wheeled Lillian into a pre-op room. We signed our consent for the surgery. I hated that she had to have surgery again. She was finally healing, and I wasn't quite ready for yet another surgery. This wasn't supposed to happen. No one had prepared me for this. Again, I was falling into a deeper depression. Lillian was breaking all of the rules. Why did no one listen to me two months ago? Why didn't the IV antibiotics and oral antibiotics kill that infection? They were very strong drugs.

A few hours later Lillian was brought back into the room. We were now in the PICU, room 2510. She was sedated and still on oxygen. The surgeon had to place a wound VAC and cut her chest back open to clean out the infection. He also needed to chip away some of her chest bone and take out two of the wires that were holding her chest bone together from the last surgery. The infection had spread to her bone, tissue, and bloodstream. We truly were lucky we caught it early.

The surgeon decided she should heal from the inside out this time, so he left her chest open. The wound VAC was placed in the opening. Its purpose is to suck out all of the germs and to help the wound heal so that it doesn't become infected again. Lillian woke up that night and looked miserable. She was swollen again and was crying. She still needed to be on oxygen. I was continually told that she requires oxygen because her little body is working so hard that it is causing her oxygen levels to drop. I was assured that as she heals, she likely will no longer need the oxygen. During surgery they also placed a PICC line. They had to prescribe stronger medicines for Lillian this time to make sure the infection did not return.

Lillian's surgery took place on my first day back to school. I was so disappointed. I did not want to miss my students' first day of school, but I had no choice. I stayed with Lillian for the first few days in the hospital. She remained an inpatient in the PICU, which made me feel comfortable and content. Nurses were always checking on her and talking to her. We remembered many of them from Lillian's first PICU stay. I decided it would be best if I returned to work the following Monday. All that the nurses were doing now was trying to wean her off oxygen and continuing to monitor her incision and wound VAC. They performed daily labs in hopes that the bacteria would quit growing on her cultures, and sure enough all the labs started to come back negative within a few days. This meant that the medicine and surgery had worked. They kept her on the medicines and planned to continue them for about four weeks.

Three days after the surgery, the nurses were having difficulty finding Lillian's pulse in her right foot. They needed to Doppler her foot to even hear a pulse, and even that was very faint. The surgeon ordered that an ultrasound of her leg be taken to determine whether a blood clot had formed. When the technician arrived, I had to help her hold Lillian's leg straight because it was difficult to perform an ultrasound on a baby so little. After finishing the ultrasound that took forever, the surgeon believed a blood clot had formed in her main artery, which had been caused by the arterial line that was placed during surgery. An ultrasound cannot detect a blood clot, so it had been pointless to have performed one. They decided to increase her heparin to make sure that the blood clot would dissolve and not travel. It seemed like so many things kept going wrong with my poor baby. Nurses had to continue to Doppler Lillian multiple times a day to listen for a pulse. By the grace of God, it slowly improved each day.

I would wake up at 4:30 am each morning and get ready for work in the hospital. Then I would kiss Lillian and head to work. I had to continue working because I knew Lillian's next surgery would take place during this school year, and I needed to save all my personal and sick days for it. I found it difficult to leave her each day. I had an hour and a half drive to work each morning. The second I would get off work, I would head straight to the hospital again. I went home only once a week to gather fresh work clothes and pack a bag. I was officially living out of a suitcase again.

I believed I was failing as both a mom and a teacher. I had to leave Preslee with my parents again while I stayed with Lillian. I was missing my big girl. For a slight moment, I had enjoyed the reality of having both of my daughters at home with me. I had been living a somewhat normal life, and now this happened. I felt like I was missing out on Preslee's life. Jeramy went to work each day, and I rarely saw him. I was doing this alone again. Granted he had to work, just as I had to work, and he had offered to stay with Lillian a couple of nights, but I didn't want to leave her. I rejected his offers to help.

One night my parents brought Preslee to the hospital. I loved getting the chance to see her. She was playing and acting silly, when out of the blue, she looked over at her grandma and called her mom. I tried not to let it bother me, but it made me sad inside. My mom corrected her and said, "No, I'm grandma." Preslee just laughed and called her mom again. I already felt like I had been neglecting her, and now she was forgetting who I was and calling her grandma "mom." I was crumbling inside. I wanted to hide in a dark hole and never come out. On one hand I felt guilty for leaving Preslee behind; on the other hand, I felt horrible for leaving Lillian in the hospital alone. I couldn't win because there was neither a right nor wrong answer to this situation. I had to do what felt right to me at the time. A few days passed, and not much had changed.

It had been reported that a total solar eclipse was supposed to happen today. Hospital staff distributed safety glasses to everyone so they could watch it. My school cancelled classes for the day because there was a risk that students might injure their eyes if they accidentally or purposefully took off their safety glasses. Plus, many parents called to say they were keeping their children home that day because they wanted to experience this phenomenal event as a family. Heavy traffic was also expected in our school district in

Farmington, Missouri, because newscasters had announced that the eclipse could be seen well in this town and the surrounding ones. Thanks to the school cancellation, I was able to stay at the hospital with Lillian. It was nice to spend an extra day with her. She was being so cute, but I could tell she was overly tired.

Shortly before the eclipse was to occur, I grabbed my safety glasses and went outside. People were pouring out of the hospital. I saw people in every direction I looked. They covered the field, the parking lot, and even the top of the parking garage. The scene reminded me of what I have always assumed I would see if the world was ending. It was so cool to experience total totality.

I was communicating with Preslee and Jeramy by phone; due to traffic, they could not make it to the hospital. Jeramy parked the car, and they watched it together while I FaceTimed them. I wish we could have watched the eclipse as a family, because it was such a neat experience and I hated having to watch it alone. As soon as it was over, I headed right back to the PICU to see Lillian. She was fast asleep. I regret that I could not carry her outside to see it, even though she was too little anyway. Preslee and Jeramy came up to the hospital that evening and brought dinner to me. Then they headed home for the night.

Jeramy and I got into an argument on the phone the next day. This whole situation was taking a harder toll on our relationship than ever before. We seldom saw each other and rarely talked. We saw things differently. He strongly suggested to me that I should leave the hospital and spend more time with Preslee. This hurt me to the core. He, too, was a heart parent. He was supposed to understand me. Instead, he was making me feel worse. I told him that I couldn't leave Lillian. He replied, "You have another daughter who needs you too." It felt like he had stabbed me in the heart with a knife. It now confirmed to me that no one, not even my husband, understood me. No one could relate to me. I started to hate myself. I hated that I was being asked to choose one daughter over the other. How could I even decide something like that? I needed to be with whichever daughter needed me the most in the moment. And in this case, it was the one who was sick. I continued to live at the hospital, go to work each morning, and return to the hospital each evening.

Lillian's incision continued to heal nicely. With each dressing change, Dr. H was very pleased with how it was healing. I learned how to pack and clean her open wound. I never thought I would have to learn how to do something like this, but I did, because I'm a heart mom now. It's just another part of this journey for which I was not prepared but was more than willing to take on. Within a week or so, we were moved back up to the TCU. This was a huge step. I was beginning to see light at the end of the tunnel.

One morning I left Lillian's room. She was finally off of oxygen and doing well. I felt comfortable to leave her to attend a heart meeting that the hospital hosts on Sunday mornings. My friend Haley would be coming up to the hospital soon, and a donut sounded tasty. I was also looking forward to meeting some other heart moms who could relate to me, and honestly, I needed a small break. I ate a donut and talked to a few heart moms. One was crying because her baby was in surgery at that very moment. She was going through a hard time. Another mom shared her heart journey with me, and I discovered that her daughter and Lillian had a lot of similarities. Although they had different heart defects, both had the same surgeon and currently were dealing with a wound VAC. Her story made me miss Lillian and I felt as though I had been gone long enough, so I decided to head back to Lillian's room.

On my way there, her nurse stopped me and said she had to put Lillian back on oxygen. She told me her levels had dropped into the 60s and weren't coming up on their own. This honestly just sucked to hear. I felt like we were backpedaling again. I walked into the room and saw that my friend Haley had arrived, along with her two boys and her mom. Haley was my blessing. She came and visited Lillian all the time. She patiently listened to me when I needed a friend to hear me. She told me that someone from cardiology had come by and was going to perform a heart scan on Lillian. This is the reason why I

126

never leave Lillian's room. Every time I do, I feel like something happens and then I regret having left. I wish I wouldn't have gotten that donut.

The Red Team came in and performed an ECHO on Lillian. They wanted to figure out why her oxygen levels kept dropping. The ECHO did not show anything. They said that her once-loud heart murmur was now faint, but the ECHO looked good. They decided to move her back to the PICU because they could not figure out what was wrong with her. Her BT shunt looked good, and her X-Ray also looked good. Down to room 2508 we went. This really stank. TCU was the light at the end of my tunnel; going back to the PICU was a big step backward. The light started to dim. I was scared and worried. This wasn't supposed to happen again.

Chapter 12
I'll Never Forgive Myself

I was happy to be back in the PICU because no one had answers for me yet as to what was wrong with Lillian. I was scared to be back here but thankful that we were in good hands. It was nice to be able to look out the PICU room door and see a group of doctors constantly staring at her monitor again. I was reassured knowing that if something happened to my daughter, they would be there. Dr. H came in and explained that they planned to simply monitor Lillian because they have no explanation as to why her oxygen levels remain low. Of course, I didn't like hearing that, but it was better for this to happen while we are in the hospital than at home. The nurses were shocked to see us back in the PICU, but all welcomed us and came in to check on Lillian. They talked about getting together again on Monday morning to discuss Lillian during the cardiac team meeting to formulate a treatment plan. They wanted to do a cardiac catheterization procedure to determine what was wrong with her heart.

Monday morning during rounds, the PICU team discussed taking Lillian back to the TCU. They said that if she was only in the PICU for oxygen, they did not see the point in keeping her there. I did not feel comfortable with this decision and made it well known. I explained to the PICU staff that I did not want her moved to a different unit until I could be there. When her cardiac team came in to check on her, I asked them if they were sending her to the TCU. They assured me that they were not sending her back to the TCU until they figured out what was wrong. This was good to hear. I told them to please discuss this with the PICU team because they had been talking about it during their rounds.

Dr. H came in while I was at work. He told Jeramy that he and the cardiology team were all in disagreement on whether or not they should do a cardiac cath on her. When looking at the risks and benefits of performing one on her, they concluded that the risks were more dangerous because her oxygen levels were so low. Since the team disagreed, this meant that the cardiac cath would not happen.

They decided to give her a blood transfusion because her hemoglobin was low. Jeramy told me that Lillian was very crabby that day. One of the nurses who we were especially fond of was there, and we knew she would be good to Lillian. Jeramy went home for the night because he had to work in the morning. I stayed with Lillian who was very irritable. I was not a huge fan of her nurse that night, as I felt she did not listen to me when I expressed concerns about Lillian. I told her repeatedly that Lillian was not acting like her usual self. She typically never cries like this and always sleeps well.

I got no sleep that night. Lillian was only happy when she was being bounced in her bouncy seat. She was impossible to console. The entire night I stayed by her bed, bouncing her. I knew I had to work in the morning and I was exhausted. At one point, Lillian started to cry and I didn't have the strength left to console her. I so badly wanted a nurse to come in and comfort her so I could sleep. I could barely work up the energy to get off the couch in her room. Nothing I did worked. But of course, no nurse came in. I picked myself up, dragged myself to Lillian's bed, and bounced her until she fell asleep.

The nurse came in at one point to check Lillian's vitals, and my baby started to cry again. I pretended like I was sleeping just to see what the nurse would do. She bounced Lillian for just a second until she stopped crying. The nurse then quickly exited the room and closed the door behind her. I couldn't believe this; it was mind-boggling. When Lillian started to cry again, I lay there for a little bit just to see if her nurse would come in and comfort her. NOPE! She never came back in. I was livid.

Although I may have been extremely tired, I was so thankful that I was at the hospital, because if I wouldn't have been, no one would have comforted my baby. This further proved to me that I needed to be there at all cost. It was another reminder that no matter how hard it gets, Lillian needs me, and I was determined not to leave her again unless I absolutely had to leave her.

I looked at the clock; 4:30 am had snuck up on me quickly. Lillian was finally sleeping. I tried to cover the bags under my eyes with some makeup. While I was applying eyeliner, Lillian's monitor sounded an alarm. I looked up to see that her heart rate was in the 60s. Then it quickly went back up to the 150s. I considered it odd but didn't put much thought into it. Shortly after, Lillian's heart rate dropped again and then quickly climbed back up. No nurse came in to check on her. I put my hair in a bun on top of my head, then pulled on a pair of black dress pants, a pair of flats, and a white dress shirt with black stripes down the middle on both sides of the buttons. I then brushed my teeth and grabbed my work bag.

Lillian's heart bradyed a few times that morning. She was sleeping, and I didn't want to wake her. I walked over to her bed and snapped a couple pictures of her on my phone. I felt so relieved that she was finally sleeping, because I was exhausted. I told her I loved her and that I would be back as soon as I got off work. I typically never take pictures of Lillian in the morning, but for some reason this morning I did.

I walked out of her room and looked down the hallway in both directions. Her nurse was nowhere in sight. No other nurses were either. I wanted to inform my nurse that Lillian's heart was bradying but figured she was being monitored 24/7, so the nurses already knew. I was running behind and couldn't be late to work. I paced back and forth across the room, aggravated, but I had to leave. I walked back into Lillian's room and whispered to her again that I loved her and would return after work. I told her I was sorry that I had to go, assuring her that the PICU was better than the TCU if I had to leave, and that they would take good care of her. I knew our favorite PICU nurse would be in at 7 am, so she would only be stuck with our invisible nurse for a couple of hours. I kissed her on the top of her head and tiptoed out of her room, being careful not to wake her up. I looked down the hallway one last time, and there was still no one in sight. I walked out of the hospital and headed to my car.

On my way to work, I stopped to buy a coffee. I never drink coffee—I don't even like coffee—but I was exhausted from getting no sleep that night and I needed something to keep me awake. My friend called me while I was driving. She was pregnant with twins and was in the hospital because she had preeclampsia. The poor girl was freaking out. I talked to her on my entire drive to work, and we even joked about how this was going to be a good day because she would get to meet her little boys. I also vented to her about how something didn't feel right with Lillian. I whined that I had gotten no sleep and was exhausted. I complained that our nurse sucked, that I couldn't believe she had shut Lillian's door so she didn't have to hear my baby cry. I told her that I was about to arrive at work, and she needed to get rest. I also said she had better send me pictures of those newborn boys the first chance she got. I was so happy for her, but I still had that feeling in the pit of my stomach that something just wasn't right regarding Lillian.

I arrived at work and started my day like any other day. All of my students were present, and the day was going smoothly. We started our reading corners, and my students were each working at their stations. I always kept my phone on me so that I could call and check on Lillian. I also wanted to always be available in case there was an emergency. At 10:16 am my phone rang, and I saw that it was the hospital. That was strange. Out of all the days I had been at work, they had never once called. I knew they were planning to take her wound VAC out, so I thought maybe that's what they were calling about. But I had a bad feeling in my stomach. Butterflies filled my stomach as I answered the phone, "Hello."

"Hi, Sarah. This is Debbie," the nurse said. Are you already at work?" I said yes. "Okay, well are you by yourself?" At this point I knew this wasn't good. My eyes instantly teared up. My legs felt wobbly, my stomach turned into knots, and I could feel the trickles of goose bumps covering my body as my gut filled with fear. "We need you to come back to the hospital," she said. We were able to get Lillian's wound VAC out early this morning; however, shortly after, Lillian's oxygen and heart rate dropped significantly low, down in the 20s. She never fully lost all of her oxygen, but we are worried. We have been doing compressions on and off for an hour, but her heart rate and oxygen levels are not rising. I'm so sorry. Dr. H is currently hooking her up to ECMO [extracorporeal membrane oxygenation]. Do you want me to call Jeramy? Do you have a ride?"

All I could focus on was the new word, ECMO. I asked her what that "e" word means. She said it's similar to life support and that she would explain it in greater detail when I got to the hospital. She told me to hang up, and she would call me back again. She wanted to make sure I was okay and needed to give me her personal cell phone number so I could reach her quickly. I was already making my way out of my classroom while we talked. I rushed to the neighboring classroom and asked the teacher to come to my room. At this point, I lost it. I rushed back into my classroom and grabbed my keys and breast pump. I tried my best to hide from my students the fact that I was crying in front of them, but I couldn't stop the river of tears. A few students asked me why I was crying. I told them that I was okay and to be good for the replacement teacher.

I left my classroom and hurried to the office, where the principal was standing by the secretaries. One look at me and she could tell that something bad had happened. All I could do was look at her. I started to cry and told her that Lillian was on life support and I had to go. She ushered me into her office, where our school counselor hugged me tight. She started to pray out loud for Lillian. I called Jeramy quickly to let him know that he had to leave work immediately. I was going to drive to him, but the principal and counselor insisted that they drive me to Jeramy. They could tell that I was in no condition to drive. It was probably a good thing because I could not focus.

I remember one of them asking if she could follow behind in my car so that both Jeremy and I had our cars with us at the hospital. I was so embarrassed by my car. It was a "good on gas" type of beater car and was trashed on the inside. There was no way I was going to let someone drive it, especially someone I worked with all the time. I insisted that I did not want them to drive it and would ask my mom to come and get it. They respectfully quit arguing with me about it. My heart was pounding out of my chest. My world was crashing down on me. To this day I have no idea what we even talked about on the way to Jeramy's workplace. I was so thankful that they drove me to him. Jeramy met me in his car and we rushed to the hospital. That hour and a half drive might as well have taken a century, because that's what it seemed like. No matter how quickly we got there, it wouldn't be quick enough for me, but we tried our best to drive safely.

On the way there, I called my mom to let her know this was an emergency. She, two of my sisters, my brother-in-law, Preslee, and Jeramy's parents met us at the hospital PICU waiting room. My mom beat Jeramy and me there. When we arrived, the first thing I did was squeeze Preslee. I was breaking inside. The tears wouldn't stop. Preslee wiped my tears and told me not to cry, which made me cry even more. I was a wreck, and everyone around me was crying too. Dr. H and the cardiac team came out to talk to me. Debbie expressed how sorry she was before telling me that Lillian was hooked to ECMO so her heart could rest. She hugged Jeramy and me and continued to talk to us. For the life of me, I can't remember what all she said. All I know is that ECMO is not good. It is used to force her blood to bypass her heart and flow into this machine to be oxygenated and put back into her body.

The cardiology team explained that they still are not certain what happened. They could not formulate a plan or strategize an approach because they didn't know exactly what was wrong with her, let alone how to fix it. I had never cried in front of these people, but for the first time ever I didn't care about hiding my emotions. I cried

… and cried … and cried. Being strong did not matter anymore. I was not strong. I was weak. I was a mess. I was mad at myself. I instinctively knew I should not have left the hospital that morning. I could feel that something was wrong. My intuition told me I should have found her nurse. My job as a heart mom is to be Lillian's voice. I was not her voice that day … and now she may die. I felt like it was all my fault.

I saw that Jeramy's grandma had posted on Facebook that Lillian was on life support and asked people to pray for her. I looked at the post and begged Jeramy to ask his grandma to take it down. There were so many people in both of our families who had not been told yet, and I didn't want them to find out on Facebook. I also did not want a ton of people trying to contact me about Lillian. I needed time to process what was going on and time to focus on Lillian. Jeramy's dad was the one to text his grandma and ask her to please remove the post. I know it seems silly to some, but I wasn't ready to answer all the questions people would ask about Lillian, and I wanted people to hear this news directly from us. It felt as though we were waiting in the PICU waiting room forever until one of the doctors from the Red Team rubbed my shoulder and asked, "Do you want to go see her?"

Chapter 13
What's the Plan?

Jeramy and I trudged slowly into room 2508. I was terrified to walk into that room. I had no idea what to expect. Time felt like it was frozen. As I walked down the narrow hallway, I thought I would never arrive at her room. I counted my breaths and could hear my heart pounding in my chest. It felt like it was slowing down, while at the same time beating so fast and hard.

As we approached Lillian's door, nurses were wheeling away coolers filled with vials of blood. They were in the process of removing these coolers from her room. This was extra blood that was left over from her ECMO. I was now more terrified than ever to walk in the room. It was freezing in there and various machines were scattered everywhere. The once very colorful room with bright pictures on the wall now looked black and white. It felt like a very dark and dreary scene from a horror movie.

I walked closer to my baby. All of the nurses just looked at us and remained very quiet. They respectfully gave us a minute to process what we were seeing. Lillian was lying on her back with her arms spread out, and her legs were bent into a frog position. She had a ventilator/ breathing machine placed down her throat. Her eyes were puffy and closed, and her little body looked pale and blue. Protruding from her neck were two full tubes of blood, which are called cannulas: One was in charge of removing the blood from her body and sending it into the ECMO machine, while the other was darker (oxygenated) blood, entering back into her body. Her heart was not beating on its own, and her lungs were not breathing on their own. The ECMO machine and the ventilator were the only things keeping her alive.

I felt Lillian's hand, and it was freezing cold. She looked and felt dead. Jeramy stood behind me and didn't say much. He placed one hand on my shoulder and just stood there. When I looked down, I saw my baby's blood splattered on the floor. I looked to my left, and her baby doll, which has brown hair and a little dress with flowers on it, was thrown under the laundry cart. She had only just received the doll a couple of days ago. Her little white and pink owl sock was missing from her foot, so she was now only wearing one sock. I could easily perceive the chaos that had taken place in room 2508 solely by looking at the room, and I had never even been there when everything was spinning out of control. I felt like I was walking on eggshells, because one wrong move by me or anyone else and my baby could die.

Lillian had a slit on her wrist with a line hanging out of it; blood seeped through the bandage that was covering it. My baby was stiff and cold. The nurses swaddled her with warm blankets in an effort to raise her body temperature. As blankets were being piled on top of her, I slid my hand under them and grabbed onto Lillian's icy foot, vigorously rubbing it and trying to warm it without success. In that moment, I felt as though my daughter was dead. I needed to warm up her foot; I needed to warm up her entire body. I couldn't stand there and do nothing. My mind was numb. How could I leave this hospital without my baby? How was I ever again going to be okay? How would I explain Lillian's death to Preslee? I talked to Lillian, telling her how very sorry I was that this had happened to her. It was killing me inside to think about how she had gone through her final hours alone. I told her how horrible of a mommy I was because I had left her, knowing in my gut that something was not right. I kissed her cold cheek and tried to hold back my tears.

Jeramy left the room so that my mom could come back in. The hospital was only allowing people to visit in pairs of two. My sister told me that as soon as Jeramy had left the room, he hugged his dad and broke down in his arms. I knew he was trying to be strong for me, but I needed to see some emotion from him. I needed to see that this was affecting him too. When Jeramy left, I was feeling alone again. My world was crumbling down on top of me, the walls were caving in, and I could barely breathe. When my mom returned to the room, she took one look at Lillian and hugged me. I could see the tears in her eyes. I told her that I had to use the restroom, when all I wanted to do was run away. I locked myself in the PICU bathroom, laid down on the dirty floor, and bawled my eyes out. I talked to God and begged him to wake me up from this nightmare, promising him that if he would just allow me to be Lillian's mommy on this Earth for a little longer and would let Lillian survive life support, then I would dedicate myself, my children, and my life to him. I promised I would start going to church and worshiping him. I needed for him to wake up Lillian.

How was I going to survive? How do I live in a world without Lillian? My heart was hurting; it was shattered. I wiped my tears after having a pity party for myself, picked myself and my broken heart off the restroom floor, and walked back to room 2508. I stared blankly through the door, then took a deep breath, and walked back into reality.

I protectively stationed myself next to Lillian, nervous as each family member came in to see her. All hands had to be washed, each visitor had to be quiet, and no one could go on the left side of her bed, which was the side on which the cannulas had been placed on her neck. If they were accidentally bumped or tugged, Lillian would bleed out onto the floor. Jeramy brought Preslee back for just a moment so that she could hug mommy and tell sissy that she loved her. I didn't want her to stay in the room long and neither did Jeramy, so he took her back to the waiting room.

I've only seen Jeramy's dad cry once before, and that was at his own father's funeral. Today, I saw him cry again. Everyone around me was terrified and crying. Lillian needed a miracle. My father-in-law was trying to hold back his tears as he told me to make sure I talk to Lillian. "She can hear you, Sarah. Talk to her. Let her know you are here and that she isn't alone." Doctors said that they needed Lillian's heart to rest so it could repair itself on its own.

They continued to perform echocardiograms to try to determine what was wrong with Lillian but could get no answers. The plan was to figure out what was wrong and then quickly fix it. But no one had answers on how to fix her. Her heart was broken, and she needed to get as much rest as possible. She was medically paralyzed, which made intubation uncomfortable, as did the ECMO procedure, and all of her cuts and bruises. The heart surgeon walked in and said he was sorry this had happened. He is a man of very few words. He didn't need to say much though because I could see in his eyes that he wanted answers and did not want to see her on that machine. He wanted her removed from it as quickly as possible, as did I. He would just stare at her in wonder while trying to figure out how to mend her. I had faith that he would.

Two nurses were required to be in the room with us constantly. One was in charge of the ECMO machine, while the other was in charge of Lillian's care. It was nerve-wracking because they would check the machine continuously to look for obvious malfunctions or any clotting. We became very close to the nurses. They were all very sweet, sympathetic, and answered every question we could think to ask. Jeramy took off work to stay with us. Preslee alternated staying with both sets of our parents. We were so thankful for the nurses, doctors, and cardiac team who had kept Lillian alive so far, but after the first day, we still had no answers.

Day one on ECMO was the hardest day of my life. I spent most of it by her bedside, crying. I kept talking to her and reminding her how strong and brave she is and how proud I was to be her mommy. I begged her to keep fighting. I was not ready to say goodbye; I needed her to be okay. I felt awful. This was the first time I truly believed I could not do a thing for her. I couldn't rescue her from this situation or take her pain away. I was broken the first time she went into cardiac arrest. I was not prepared for it and thought it would be the hardest thing I would ever have to witness. I was wrong, but still, this was killing me inside. I felt numb and broken. I would have done anything to switch places with her.

It was crowded in the room with the two nurses, the ECMO machine, and all of the other instruments and

IV poles. We were never alone in the room; we had no privacy at all. I loved this because I was assured the hospital staff was watching over Lillian very carefully, but it was also stressful because we were never alone to grieve.

The nurses were all nice. We couldn't begin to know how to thank them enough. There was nothing to do in the room other than sit there and pray. I prayed for God to guide the surgeon's hands as he attempted to repair her heart and to let us wake up from this nightmare. I couldn't imagine living a life without her. The nurses helped to distract me at some points throughout this bad dream, as they were very friendly and talked to us when they weren't in the middle of helping with a crisis. We talked about life, our children, camping, and the outdoors. Some of them complimented me on how strong I was and what devoted parents Jeramy and I were to Lillian. They said my family was sweet and that Lillian was blessed that God had gifted her to us. They helped shine some light on our situation, but it was still killing me.

We joked about how the coffee shop downstairs was always closed and how the nurses were not allowed to use their coffee machine for patients and their families. They said there was a Keurig but never any coffee pods to go along with it. I wanted to show my appreciation to them and purchase coffee pods for their break room, but I needed to wait on that until Lillian was removed from life support. We always put together gift baskets as a way to say thank you to our nurses and cardiac team and give a special gift to her heart surgeon. The only problem was that this time the surgery would not be planned. None of this was planned. For now, my thank-you gifts were placed on hold because I would not be able to make them.

At one point, I sat down on the couch in our room and started scrolling through pictures on my phone. The doctors were not giving us much hope. They were clueless as to what was wrong with Lillian or how to treat her. I couldn't believe that my baby was lying there practically dead and all I could do was watch in horror. The pictures made me cry even harder. In my mind I planned which pictures I would use in a slideshow for her funeral and contemplated where I would lay her to rest. I was angry at God, and I was angry at life. If Lillian didn't survive, then I didn't want to live either. I'm what could be considered a "flight from fright" kind of girl. When I think I can't handle a frightening situation, my first thought is to take flight and run away. I couldn't flee from my nightmare this time, but by the same token, I couldn't live with it either.

At one point I thought all I have to do is swallow a bunch of pills and fall asleep. I wouldn't have to wake up and continue to live this nightmare. Suicidal thoughts crossed my mind a couple of times, but now I am thankful I didn't follow through. I praise God for stopping me. I didn't really want to die; I just wanted the heartache and pain to go away, to be able to fall asleep and not wake up in the hospital. I wanted my baby girl to not have to endure such big obstacles. Life wasn't fair.

Suicide would never have solved my problems or those of my baby. The strange thing is, when one thinks about suicide, she is thinking only of herself—at least that was the case for me. I was a coward, but I am so grateful to the Lord for rescuing me from these thoughts. Preslee's face entered my mind. It wouldn't be fair to her, as she was already going through so much. I couldn't do this to her. She, and the little hope I had left in me that Lillian would live, kept me alive, and God ultimately saved my life. This baby had also been through more than her fair share of difficulties. Why did her heart have to be broken? Why did I have to have a miscarriage and then have a baby who has congenital heart disease? But I wouldn't have changed it for the world. This baby girl was my hero, but I wanted to be her hero for a change and couldn't. I began to shut out the world again.

That night I decided to reach out to our friends and family to pray for Lillian. A couple of months earlier, I had created a Facebook page to keep them informed about her progress, or lack thereof. I was exhausted with having to repeatedly answer the same questions. My primary intent was to avoid forgetting to tell someone who needed to know. I named the page

"Love for Lillian." We received about sixty likes on the page, all of which were from out-of-town family, in-town family, and close friends. I did not want people to have to hear news through the grapevine, so I created a post that read:

"It breaks my heart to even have to post this, but Lillian is on Life Support. At 10:16 am I received a phone call from the hospital to come back to the hospital.... I was at work. She stated that Lillian's heart rate and oxygen dropped extremely low (in the 20s and 30s) and would not come back up. They started compressions. They did compressions on and off for 1 hour while her surgeon started the procedure to put her on the ECMO machine. She is intubated again and currently medically paralyzed. The real struggle is that they have no answers. They have no idea what is wrong with her. They keep looking at the shunt and her but can't figure it out. You can tell her heart surgeon is becoming frustrated. They keep doing EKGs, Echoes, and ultrasounds on her. They think her shunt may be blocked, but it looks like it's still pushing blood through, so it makes no sense. This has to be the hardest day of my life thus far. No answers. The world would be such a dark place without Lillian's smile. Seeing her just lying there and all these cords and what not hooked to her is painful. They plan to keep her comfy and resting for a little while. They don't want her on this machine for too

long as there are complications that come with it. I feel like my world is crumbling down on me. Things change so quickly with this heart warrior. Prayers are appreciated!

This post was difficult to write but turned out to be a blessing in disguise. Within one day, it was shared over 450 times. There were over 1,000 likes on it and over 1,100 comments. People from all over the country were praying for Lillian and my family. I read every single comment on that post, which helped to keep my mind busy. It was so nice to read all of the encouraging words and prayers being said for my family and my beautiful baby girl. I also started to receive messages through Lillian's page. In one night, we had almost 2,000 likes on our page! I was astonished that so many people wanted to know more about Lillian and pray for her, people who cared and were thinking about my baby girl. It was amazing to see the love pour in for Lillian and our family.

I received a message on Facebook from a woman who was actually present in the PICU when Lillian went into cardiac arrest. She said that she was praying for Lillian and informed me that Lillian's surgeon had been in the middle of performing another heart surgery on another patient when Lillian coded. This woman said she was aware that I had not been there but, if it would make me feel any better, every available doctor and nurse had flocked to Lillian's room. Not one single medical professional remained in the halls at that time. They were all in Lillian's room, trying to save her life. She told me that she had prayed for Lillian the entire time. I needed to hear this so badly. I had blamed myself for leaving that morning; I was so mad at myself. I could not believe that my daughter was without me when this had happened. I was dying inside, but it gave me some satisfaction to know that Lillian was not completely alone.

The next day there was nothing new to report. Lillian was still on life support, and her heart was still not functioning well enough to perform a procedure to try to save her. They decided to let her rest for the remainder of the day and give her heart more time to heal. The good news was that her heart appeared a little stronger and her kidneys were still working. I walked to the water machine to get something to drink and to use the restroom.

I saw a mom who looked familiar. I had been following a Facebook page of a little girl with Trisomy 18, a condition caused by an error in cell division. I always thought how amazingly strong this little baby was and how much strength her mommy must have herself. I was right; it was this mom I had been seeing. I knew her daughter was in the PICU, fighting off a virus. She looked exhausted. I greeted her and let her know that I was praying for her daughter. I knew she was searching for breastmilk at one point, so I asked her if she still needed some. She explained that her baby had to start formula but thanked me for the offer. We talked some more, and she told me where I could find the mom who I originally had been trying to find. She said she had heard about Lillian because the baby who was left on the operating table when Lillian coded also had Trisomy 18 and her mother was a friend. She gave me her friend's name so that I could write to her.

I wrote her friend a message on Facebook that night to let her know I was sorry that Dr. H had to leave her daughter on the operating table to save my daughter's life. I said I could not imagine how she must have been feeling while waiting for her daughter's surgery to be completed and then receiving a call telling her that her child's surgeon had to leave in the middle of the operation. I told her that I had prayed for her daughter's surgery to go well at the time, and I would continue to pray for her. She wrote me back to tell me how sorry she was about Lillian. She said she knew that things did not look good for someone's baby when the alarms went off in the PICU, even though she hadn't known the infant was my baby. She realized that a baby was being put on life support, and she was very sorry. She was so sweet, and we continued to share our stories and talk to each other through Facebook for a while. It felt nice to have another person to relate to and talk to who understands what it's like to have a baby with a serious illness. I especially needed it in that moment because I was feeling very alone.

We started to receive care packages in the mail and at the hospital from random people. An old high school teacher of mine sent me a bag full of snacks, coloring books, gifts for Preslee, and the sweetest card. Another heart mom dropped off a basket of drinks, a journal, snacks, and small items we could use at the hospital. The family that we met in the hospital during Lillian's first surgery, the beautiful girl with curly hair who Preslee loved and became friends with, sent us a sound and light machine. Her mom told me that her daughter slept very well with it, which helped her to get some rest too. The community outreach helped to shine light on my dark reality. Although it didn't take away the pain I was feeling knowing that my daughter may die, it certainly helped to give me hope in what was oftentimes becoming a crazy world. People's prayers were working. Those who I knew, and even those who I had never met, were sending their deepest thoughts and prayers to my family.

I would randomly scroll through Facebook, because there wasn't much else happening. Many people were simply going about their daily lives as if they didn't have a care in the world: sharing pictures of their happy kids, reporting some occasional drama, or just posting about how their day was going. I looked out the window of our PICU room and watched people enter and exit the hospital. I watched folks driving in their cars and kids happily running around and playing. But me, I was in a dark and cold hospital room while everyone was living life. Why are people complaining about politics, about work, about how their kids are acting? I just wanted my baby awake, off life support, breathing on her own, and having a mended heart. Everyone's life was going on, but mine was frozen in time. My life felt like it was ending while I waited and prayed that Lillian would survive another day.

That night one of the nurses noticed that Lillian's arm was shaking a little. They hooked her up to an electroencephalography test (EEG), which measures electrical activity of the brain, to make sure she was not having a seizure, which is a common side effect of ECMO. All I knew was that if she was having a seizure, it was not going to be good. It took forever for them to hook her up. Glue was now stuck everywhere on her hair. She had wires and tape everywhere, and I could barely see her scalp. She looked like an alien hooked to all of the wires. This was very difficult for me to look at. I was terrified, thinking Lillian could be having a seizure. Praise God it was not a seizure and that the EEG was not recording any other signs of strokes or seizures. They unhooked her after an hour.

Jeramy's brother came to visit Lillian in the hospital. I did not want any kids there because we had to be extremely careful around Lillian. As I mentioned previously, we were not allowed on one side of her bed because that is where the cannulas were and they could not be tugged on. If they fell out of her neck or became unplugged from the machine, she would bleed out and die. This meant I did not want to chance anything; having kids there would be dangerous and would add to my stress. Jeramy's brother brought his son. I tried hard not to be angry. I knew he didn't have a babysitter but still wanted to see Lillian. It was a tough situation. I kept finding myself in these difficult situations, and it was frustrating. Understandably, Jeramy's nephew was bored, so I had to keep my eye on him.

The small room was packed with machines, nurses, and now visitors. There was nothing for Jeramy's nephew to do after his tablet died. He got up off of the couch to run to his dad and tripped over one of the cords on the floor. This cord just so happened to be the plug for Lillian's ECMO machine. The plug was pulled from the wall and my heart dropped. I jumped up quickly and shouted, "He unplugged her life support machine!" I was finished. It wasn't the boy's fault; it was an accident, but I couldn't take it anymore. This all was too much. Thank God the machine is on a battery and the nurse quickly plugged it back in. I wanted everyone to leave. I wanted to be left alone. I had reached my breaking point and had shut down inside.

Chapter 14
Her Heart Looks Repaired Enough

The next morning, the cardiac team came in and completed another ECHO on Lillian's heart. They confirmed that her heart looked as if it had repaired itself enough. They believed that Lillian's BT shunt had clotted and been shattered during compressions. The only option to remove her from ECMO was to place another BT shunt. They explained to us that they could not enter through her chest now because of an infection, and they needed that site to heal completely. They planned to cut open her right side and enter through her rib cage. The cardiac team was not certain this would work, as the reason for why she had gone into cardiac arrest was still not one hundred percent clear.

Jeramy asked them what their plan was if this did not work. Their response was that there was no other option, no plan B. They were hopeful this would work, but hopeful isn't certain. While they were preparing the operating room, I thought about those words. I was more afraid now than ever before. I didn't want this moment to be the last one I had with my daughter. I didn't want Lillian to pass away and have this be the last image I would ever have of her. There had to be more they could do. Lillian was not born to go through all of this and not survive it. Nothing seemed fair. I hoped that my baby could hear me, so I tried hard not to cry.

I talked to Lillian and told her how much I loved her. I reminded her how much I needed her in my life. I didn't want to say goodbye and told her again how strong and brave she was while I kissed her freezing cold head. I kissed her little bruised stomach and rubbed her tiny legs and feet. I had to touch her. I didn't know if this would be my last time to see her somewhat alive. I knew if I stood there too long, I would break down. I had to stay strong for her because that's what she needed right now. But inside, I was breaking. I thought I was saying my goodbyes.

Today was also Lillian's three-month birthday. The family crisis nurse came in and painted Lillian's feet and then placed her footprints on the canvas three times each. When she handed me the picture, I saw three little pink and purple butterflies the nurse had made with Lillian's feet. This was breathtaking. The three butterflies represented each month of Lillian's life. I cried looking at it, thinking these could be the last footprints I'll ever have of Lillian, the only artwork I would ever receive of my baby. This was the most beautiful gift she could have given to me. I put it on the shelf in Lillian's PICU room, which added some bright color to a very dark situation. Any time someone entered the room, he or she would see Lillian's bright purple and pink footprints.

My sisters came up and decorated Lillian's PICU room door. They placed her name in wooden letters at the top of the door. They had pictures printed from Lillian's newborn photos, which had been taken the first time she went home.

One of the pictures was of Lillian lying on her blanket that reads, "God Knew My Heart Needed You." I had bought this blanket when I found out I was pregnant with my rainbow baby. God knew my heart needed this baby. During my maternity photos, I used this blanket to represent my acknowledgement that even though this baby would be born with a heart condition, God knew I would need this baby in my heart and in my life. Lillian made my heart whole when she was born. And even though this was a terrifying moment in my life and I was falling apart, this picture reminded me that God knew my heart needed Lillian. I was forever changed. I am a better person and have a bigger heart because of Lillian. I desperately needed this reminder. I owe my life to God now. He has proven to me time and time again that he loves me and my family. And ultimately, God knows my heart needs him.

I prayed so hard in that moment and apologized

to God for not praying very often before. I promised him
that day that if he would let Lillian live, I would try to be
a better person, to go to church, and to pray more often.
Although I did not grow up a super religious person, I
believed in God now more than ever before. I was
leaving this up to him.

Lillian's door was beautiful just like her, and it
helped to shine some light on the situation. Any time I
would leave this room and come back in, I would never
see an empty door. I will always be reminded of what a
strong three-month-old heart baby God gave me.
Whenever anyone walks past her door, they will know a
heart warrior had been fighting big battles in this room
and that she is beautiful and loved. I was so proud of her,
and looking at this door reminded me constantly of how
far she has come. It made me smile every time someone
stopped by the door and looked at my baby's pictures.

A group of doctors and nurses came in to
Lillian's room. They were referred to as the "Purple
Team." There were so many of them because it takes an
army of people to transfer her to the operating room with
her ECMO machine. They had to be very careful and
watch every move because they could not accidentally
unhook her from this machine, and they also had to be
careful that the cannulas did not get bumped. They
surrounded her bed, hooked up her oxygen tank, adjusted
all of the wires, and hooked her monitor to the portable
one for her bed. I sat on the couch in room 2508, just

watching everything they were doing. I prayed so hard in that moment that I would see my baby again. They had no other plan, which still terrified me. Jeramy kissed Lillian on the head and told her he loved her. I couldn't do it. I was not going to say goodbye. I sat on that couch and didn't move, clinging to Lillian's stuffed animals. I hugged them tight as a tear rolled down my cheek. I held her turtle WubbaNub binky in my hand and stared at it, praying I would get to see her suck on it again. They wheeled Lillian out of the room, taking up the entire hallway with her machines and bed. I was now in an empty room. It felt so cold and wrong. I had to get out of there.

Chapter 15
Her Heart Is Beating on Its Own

We decided to wait at the Ronald McDonald house again. I created a Facebook post on the "Love for Lillian" page, and people I didn't even know began praying for Lillian. This helped me tremendously, as I could feel the love pouring in from everywhere. With so many people praying, God had to hear these prayers! For the first time in a long time I felt hope.

My sister created a page to solicit donations to cover Lillian's medical expenses. Numerous people were donating money, saying kind words, and praying for Lillian and my family. The financial burden associated with raising a heart warrior can be overwhelming, and we could not afford to pay these expensive hospital bills. Many generous people donated money over the first few days, and we raised almost enough to pay our deductible and out-of-pocket expenses. This was now one less thing I had to worry about. God works in brilliant and mysterious ways. People enter our lives when we least expect them to because they are angels sent from God, and we are forever grateful that he sent lots and lots of angels on Lillian's behalf.

It was an extremely long five hours waiting to receive the call that would tell us whether Lillian would live or die. I kept my phone glued to my hand. Every so often we would get a call to let us know how surgery was progressing; hospital staff kept us informed each step of the way. We watched TV while I tried to eat something, even though nothing seemed appetizing. I struggled with doing simple daily activities because the thought that my daughter might not make it out of surgery alive kept racing through my mind.

Every ounce of my body was weak and hurting. I felt like I was dying inside, but there wasn't a thing I could do about it. I would randomly tear up and feel sick to my stomach. Everything about that day was a fog. I struggle to recall details now because my mind had been wandering off to dark places that day. At around 5 pm, we received a call telling us that Lillian's heart was beating on its own again and to head back to the PICU waiting room so that her heart surgeon could give us a brief summary of the surgery. All we knew was that her new BT shunt had been placed successfully and she had done well. She had returned to the operating room at 12:30 pm, and surgeons began closing up her wound around 5 pm.

Dr. H met with us around 5:45 pm and was happy to tell us that Lillian was doing well and was able to come off of ECMO easily. He could not remove the old BT shunt, however, because it was impossible to reach through her side. He informed us that he would remove both shunts when she was big enough and healthy enough to withstand a full heart repair. Overall, he was very pleased with how things were looking. We were relieved to hear this and could not admire him more for his outstanding surgical ability. He is the reason Lillian is still with us. I will never find the right words to express how grateful I am that he kept her alive. Words for something this marvelous and extraordinary have not been invented yet. He is forever a hero in my eyes, and I will love him forever.

While I was sitting in the waiting room, I read a message on Facebook from a very sweet mom who asked if she could bring dinner to us. I didn't know much about her, but she was insistent and I was not about to turn down an offer of food. I was tired of hospital food. She came and dropped off a bag full of food along with a blue bag. She hugged me and told me that we were in her thoughts and prayers. She also presented me with a second bag and requested that I deliver it to the mom I had met the day Lillian went on life support, the one whose daughter has Trisomy 18. She reinforced my own view that giving gifts to others will also put a smile on my face.

After she left I opened the blue bag. Inside was a very soft blanket and heart leg warmers for Lillian, a gift card for gas, gift cards to restaurants, snacks, and a variety of other goodies. At the bottom of the bag lay a little card with a picture of a boy on it. This mom was a heart mom and I had no idea. Her little boy had fought a courageous battle against CHD but sadly had lost the fight after getting the flu. It became her mission to raise awareness of and shine light on families who were going through a tough time with their hospitalized heart warriors. My heart sank for her and I felt guilty for a moment. What a beautiful and thoughtful thing for her to do. Her poor son had already earned his wings, yet here she was trying to make other heart moms smile. Tears rolled down my face as I looked at the picture of this sweet, beautiful little boy who had fought such a hard battle. God had gifted me with another angel who I will forever cherish. I said a prayer in that moment and thanked him for not taking my daughter from me.

It was finally time for me to see Lillian. It was so hard to see her hooked up to all of the machines again. As before, she was very swollen and did not look like my baby. I felt awful for her. She had earned some new scars that she would proudly wear for the rest of her life. She has scars on her neck, wrist, chest, and side that will heal with time but will never completely disappear. They are gorgeous beauty marks that I am proud of because they display her strength and bravery, but they also sadden me because they are reminders of every battle she has had to face.

Lillian was intubated again and not allowed to breathe on her own yet. Her room looked so much bigger now that the ECMO machine had been removed. It was such a relief to see that she no longer required life support. We were thankful for everyone's prayers. Although she was still not one hundred percent in the clear yet, she was doing quite well. Doctors were mildly concerned about the incision in her neck caused by the cannulas when they had to refry the vessels. They were carefully monitoring them because they continued to bleed; otherwise, everything was going pretty smoothly. They kept her intubated and medically paralyzed so that she could rest. She had a few rough days and they did not want to rush anything, so they let her continue to rest the next day as well.

Once Lillian was awake enough, she was extubated. She now only required a little oxygen because, for the most part, she was breathing on her own. She appeared to be slightly uncomfortable, so nurses continued to give her pain medicine. Packages and gift cards were still pouring in. People from my work brought gifts for both of my daughters and raised quite a bit of money to help cover Lillian's medical expenses, while a church near my work also raised a significant amount of money. We could feel the love people had for Lillian and our family, and we greatly appreciated their support. People were very generous, and for the first time ever I felt like we could stop worrying about hospital bills and our dire financial situation. Sadly, the days I spent with Lillian were unpaid work days for me because I had already used all of my sick time and personal days. When Lillian was placed on life support, I promised her that I would never leave her again while she is in the hospital. These donations helped me to keep that promise.

Four days after Lillian's surgery, I was finally able to hold her again. It felt good to have her in my arms. I hadn't held her since she had been placed on ECMO two weeks ago. I had feared that I would never get to enjoy this moment with her again and vowed never to take something so precious for granted. I was filled with a whirlwind of emotion. Her drainage lines had been pulled and she was placed on an NG feeding tube again. Doctors were careful to monitor Lillian closely because they were concerned that her lung might collapse due to her enlarged diaphragm, and if this happened, they might have to perform another surgery. They were optimistic that it would just repair itself. Respiratory staff started working with her every four hours to help break up the gunk in her chest. Daddy also got to hold Lillian today. It was refreshing to finally start to feel like parents again. This helped to ease my depression. Jeramy stayed at the hospital with me each day. It was gratifying to have him there because it showed me that he cared and wanted to be there for his daughter.

On day five, there was talk of moving Lillian back to the TCU. This meant that we would be one step closer to going home! However, we can't forget that Lillian is notorious for breaking all the rules. We all know by now that she does things her own little Lillian way. One step forward always resulted in two steps back. Lillian had been assigned a training nurse that day, and she came into the room to assess our baby. Lillian's oxygen levels had dropped, so the trainee nurse walked over to the oxygen machine and turned it up for a minute and the oxygen levels climbed back up. I asked her what happened, and she said that Lillian just needed a little extra oxygen. Something did not feel right about this, even though it appeared to have worked.

I was talking to Lillian and she was giving me the cutest smiles ever. She was lying in bed and her big gummy smiles were melting my heart. Then, all of a sudden, my baby stopped smiling. I looked at the machines that were now sounding their alarms. Lillian was turning blue and was unresponsive. Jeramy came over to the bed and waved his hand in front of her eyes. Nothing. He then ran into the hallway to find a nurse. The nurse came in and asked what happened, and then she, too, turned up Lillian's oxygen. We explained to her what had occurred. She agreed that it was weird, but turning up the oxygen worked again. She called the doctors to let them know. We told her that the trainee nurse had done the same thing about an hour prior to this episode. This nurse had not been made aware of it, which made me angry. The trainee nurse had not told anyone!

Lillian started to have episodes in which her oxygen levels would drop into the low 20s and 30s. When this happens, she seems to freeze and turn blue for twenty seconds or so. After the third episode, nurses had to place a respirator bag on her, in addition to turning up her oxygen, to get her breathing again. This is called "bagging." They were not sure why this was happening. Dr. H came in and ordered that an ECHO be performed. When he comes into Lillian's room now, he just stares at her with his hand on his chin. He always looks confused and stumped by what to do for her and doesn't understand why she is breaking all the rules. Either way we are confident that he will do whatever it takes to find answers and won't stop until he finds them. I'm always at peace, knowing Dr. H is there. Lillian's shunt looks good now. They hooked her up to an EEG and talked about intubating her again. They thought that this was only Lillian's second episode because the trainee nurse had never reported the first one. I had to keep reminding them that this was actually the third episode.

It was scary to watch all this happen. One moment Lillian would be smiling and happy, and the next she would stare off into space and her oxygen levels would drop. After three episodes, we started timing each individual occurrence. Every forty minutes, she would have another episode. The EEG gave her a mummy-like appearance. It was an adorable look on her but still very scary. It took forever to hook her up. She had a few more episodes, but sadly the EEG was not registering them. It became a mystery as to why this was occurring. Lillian was exhausted. Every forty minutes her alarm would go off and the doctors and nurses in the PICU would come running. We had to watch them bag her five times. It was terrifying. Lillian's heart surgeon came in demanding answers, but no one had them. The PICU team deemed her as having seizures, but the neurology staff did not want to say for certain that's what it was since the EEG wasn't picking them up. After seven seizures it became apparent to them that they had to do something. One of the PICU doctors decided to place her on Keppra, a seizure medicine, and she never had another episode.

Two days later Lillian was completely off of oxygen and CPAP, having not experienced another seizure since starting Keppra. The technician performed an MRI (a scan that shows the brain) on her, which showed she had a thin layer of blood on the left side of her brain and some white matter/hemorrhage in her brain. We were told this is common when a patient is on ECMO. Someone from neurology said that her brain should absorb the blood, but there is no way to

167

determine if this would affect her in the future. Lillian struggled with eating today. She had been coughing a lot and choking a little on her bottles. The doctor ordered that a swallow study be performed on her to rule out some things.

This hospital has become our second home. We have grown very close to many of the nurses who have made our stay more bearable. I love the way they talk to Lillian, rub her hair, and genuinely care about her. One of our favorite TCU nurses, Lillian's birthday buddy, keeps coming down to the PICU to check on her and to leave cute notes. It makes me so happy to see all of the talented nurses in the PICU, TCU, and on the cardiology team love on Lillian. They take such great care of her, and we are forever thankful. Lillian's swallow study test came back fine. It was determined that she just has a lot of gunk in her lungs and that a slow flow nipple would be best for her. She is still receiving her breathing treatments to break up the gunk and help with her cough.

I remembered that I was not able to give my thank-you gifts. Now that Lillian was doing a little better, I needed to thank the people who have kept her alive. I recalled the conversation I had with our nurses about coffee and sent Jeramy to the store to purchase a huge box of Keurig coffee cups. I also wrote a thank-you card to Dr. H and gave him a Starbucks gift card because he always drank coffee during his morning rounds. I can never do enough to show my appreciation for this man, so I hope my words help him to understand how grateful we are to him for saving our daughter. We bought M&M's for the PICU doctors because the vending machine that dispensed M&M's always seemed to be empty. Our room was directly across from the doctors and all the computer screens. I would watch them walk to the vending machine to try to get candy, but the machine was seldom stocked. I wanted to refill it for them, so we bought a huge bag of M&M's and Peanut M&M's. We also bought snacks and frappés for the Red Team. I traditionally personalize these gifts to make them more meaningful, but under these circumstances, this just wasn't possible. I was happy that I could do *something* for them even though what I was capable of doing seemed small, especially considering that I credit them with saving my baby's life and know they deserve so much more.

Lillian was starting to do better, so Jeramy returned to work. He would visit at nighttime and spend the day with us when he wasn't scheduled to work. Preslee was still staying with my parents. Because Lillian's health was taking a turn for the better, I was happier. Jeramy mentioned that I should go visit our friend's twin babies who were born on the day that Lillian went on life support. They were adorable and I wanted to meet them, but I had promised Lillian I would not leave her until she was discharged from the hospital and back home. It angered me that Jeramy was always trying to get me to leave. Yes, he was trying to help me out and had even said that he would stay with Lillian while I was gone, but I just couldn't go. I was becoming very annoyed with him. How on Earth can he expect me to leave my baby? Why can't he just take no for an answer? Maybe I should have taken a break from the hospital, but I had made a promise to my daughter and a promise is a promise.

Chapter 16
Here We Go Again

Eight days after Lillian received her new shunt and was removed from ECMO, she was finally being transferred to the TCU. This meant we were one step closer to going home. I was afraid to tell anyone because I didn't want to jinx her, but it was finally happening. I couldn't help but stop to reflect on the crazy journey we have been on with Lillian. She is such a trooper, and I am very proud to be her mommy, but I don't feel I deserve to have someone so precious in my life. I may never know the reason why God chose me to guide her through life—and to support, encourage, and love her— but I thanked him wholeheartedly in that moment for doing the one thing I couldn't do: protect her. She has been put through the wringer over and over again, yet she continues to smile through it all. She is stronger than me, braver than me, and a better person than me, and she is only three months old. She is not merely a warrior; she is a baby of mystery ... a true living legend.

We have spent so much time in the PICU lately, and honestly, I'd rather be anyplace but here. The waiting room is always full of people sleeping, eating, talking, and crying. The crying is hardest to watch. Parents and family members go through a plethora of emotions. It is heart-wrenching to see families practically living there. I encountered many different people dealing with many different problems. One day, when we were waiting for nurses to change a bandage on Lillian and replace it with a sterile one, I saw a family that I had been watching for a week, and they were crying and obviously frustrated. An older woman was arguing with a younger man who appeared to be her son. As they continued to quarrel, I heard that his daughter had become ill. His family thought he had waited too long to take her to the hospital. They were going back to the girl's hospital room in pairs of two.

Each time a pair would return to the waiting room from the PICU, they would be crying. I knew that whatever was happening back there could not be good. The man I assumed to be the girl's father ran out of the waiting room and everyone was crying. I saw them begin to wheel all of their belongings out of the waiting room; they had a lot of stuff to remove because they had practically lived there for a week. The waiting room was now silent. Everyone was gone … except us.

Later that day I learned that a little girl had passed away. My sister-in-law shared a post that asked people to pray for the child, and I was able to connect the dots. I messaged the girl's dad and told him how sorry I was for his loss and that I was praying for his family. I explained how I had found out about his daughter and shared that my daughter has been in the PICU for a month. He wrote back, and his message was very sweet. I saw so much heartache and heard so much anguish in the PICU that it tore me up inside. But I saw and heard good things as well, and I tried to focus on those. I was relieved and happy to be moving to the TCU.

Lillian slowly started to eat better. The incision on her chest was healing nicely and no longer needed to be packed. Now we only had to apply saline, gauze, and tape to her wounds. For the first time in a long time, I cried happy tears. I couldn't help but cry when I looked at her sweet smile, a smile that I was terrified I'd never get to see again. It has been a very emotional month with twists and turns for which I was not prepared. I was missing Preslee more than anything, and my world was crumbling all around me. My heart and body ached. I can never explain the unbearable pain that filled my body on August 29, 2017, when Lillian went on life support. But here she is a week and a half later, smiling, and that smile means more to me than she will ever know. She had beaten the odds. I still have a million fears and will forever be a super paranoid and an overprotective mom, but she inspires me to be a better person. Her strength is admirable and her smile is breathtaking and contagious.

The next day Lillian looked happy to finally have her NG tube removed. She was now eating enough that it was no longer required. But it wasn't always easy to get her to eat enough, and there were moments when I really had to work at it, but each bottle was another step forward. She was making progress and getting stronger each day. All of her incisions were healing nicely, she started sleeping well again, and she faced each new day like a champ. Speech therapy and respiratory staff were still coming in, which helped her continue to improve. For some reason, each time the NG tube is removed, Lillian decides she doesn't want to eat anymore. She is such a little stinker! The only thing still keeping us in the hospital was the fact that she still had her PICC line and doctors wanted to continue to monitor how much she was eating.

As the next couple of days dragged by, I was becoming more and more impatient. We were slowly creeping up on a month's stay this time, and I was exhausted. I wanted to be home with Lillian and Preslee and get back to feeling somewhat sane again. I especially feared having to return to work. Everything that had happened since Lillian was born was almost always unplanned and unexpected. No one had prepared me for the battles we were facing. I was mentally, physically, and emotionally drained. I kept reflecting on happier moments that had occurred during the short amount of time when Lillian had been home. We had now lived in a hospital more days than we had lived at home. This is what being a heart mom is all about; this drama had become our new life. We were ready for Preslee to be with her sissy again because she adores and loves Lillian so much.

Dr. H came in daily to check on Lillian. From a heart standpoint, she was doing amazing, but he asked someone from the department of infectious diseases to come in and evaluate her. The medication she was taking for her infection had to be administered via a PICC line, so there was talk about sending us home with it. I am already skilled at giving PICC line medications because Jeramy has cystic fibrosis and has required a PICC line twice since we have been together. At age sixteen I learned how to flush a PICC line with saline, how to put heparin in the line to prevent clotting, how to hook him to a drip line and ensure that the line is properly placed in regard to gravity flow for the duration of the medication being dispensed, how to get air out of the line, and how to mix the medications. I was becoming a nurse, which is something I have never wanted to be. The sight of blood used to make me quiver in fear that I would pass out. I had seen blood everywhere during the past three months, so I don't even flinch at the sight of it anymore, having seen so much worse.

I was okay with going home with the PICC line, but it was not ideal. After many conversations with staff from infectious diseases, they were able to substitute the PICC line medication with an oral antibiotic, which Lillian was required to take for four more days. Dr. H wanted us out of the hospital. He does not like for a heart patient to remain in the hospital any longer than necessary because there are a lot of sick people there. One thing a lot of people don't seem to understand is how dangerous a normal sickness and cold can be to a heart warrior. Germs can be detrimental to them. Lillian would be discharged the next day as long as everything looked okay on her ECHO and EKG. We were excited that Dr H. wanted Lillian out of the hospital. We were more than ready to take our daughter home.

The next morning I woke up early and packed our bags. Lillian's room was full of gifts, snacks, clothes, and necessities. On this stay we had lived in the hospital for thirty days, and today was the day our baby would be discharged. The technician came in and completed her ECHO and EKG and said everything looked great. A nurse listened to her pulse to make sure the blood clot that had formed before ECMO had improved, and an X-Ray was taken to check her diaphragm. Everything looked as it should.

The nurses had Lillian's medications filled at the pharmacy so that we would have everything we needed to go home. I, the mother who milks like a cow, had stockpiled way too much breast milk at the hospital during this 30-day stay because I had so much that I decided to be a milk donor a week ago. I reminded the nurses of this and told them that I did not want to take any of the milk home, to please donate it to the hospital's NICU. I knew I had no room in my freezer at home to store a milk factory's worth of milk. The nurses could not believe that I had been at the hospital for only a month and had donated over one thousand ounces of milk. We said our goodbyes to our favorite nurses, reviewed the discharge paperwork, and busted out of Lillian's prison.

I was excited to finally be leaving with my baby girl. I had waited for what seemed like forever for this precious Kodak moment. I had been terrified thinking this day would never come, and yet here we are sitting in the car in the hospital parking lot. I am leery of pulling away. What if something happens to Lillian when I get home? What if my baby stops breathing while she's asleep? What if I don't notice because I'm sleeping too? This was just the beginning of many sleepless nights in which I was plagued by new and unfounded fears. As I drove out of the parking lot with Lillian in the back seat, happy tears rolled down my face. It had been a while since I'd been outside, and today the sun was shining. It felt good to get some sun. I reminisced about everything Lillian had been through, took a deep breath, and continued to drive. I was more than ready to go and get Preslee. I missed my older baby girl so much.

I pulled into my mom's driveway, quickly picked up Preslee, and headed straight home. My normally clean and neat house had been destroyed. Toys were scattered everywhere. I was not happy to come home to such a mess. I wished so badly that my husband would have cleaned everything up so I didn't have to stress about it, but I thought, it is what it is. I loved on both of my girls for a bit, while growing increasingly irritated that I had to clean up after a tsunami-level disaster had taken place during Lillian's 30-day stay in the hospital. Jeramy's mom visited for a while, and Jeramy was also home for a few days. This meant that Preslee was home, and boy, did she make a mess. No one helped clean up the messes. What probably frustrated me the most was that my husband had said on several different nights that he was going home a little early because he had to clean up the house. That house was nowhere near clean. This was the last thing I wanted to stress about on my first day home, but I took a deep breath and I cleaned. And then I cleaned some more. I didn't want Lillian to live in a messy house, or Preslee either for that matter. I decided to take the last couple of days of the week off work to adjust to being home and to take Lillian to her follow-up appointments. I returned to work the following week.

Going back to work was hard. I struggled to get any sleep. I was terrified to leave Lillian, but her Maw-

Maw would be watching her, so I knew she was in amazingly capable hands. I was ready to be back at school with my sweet first graders, but I was not prepared to be away from my girls yet. I found it difficult to return to work and actually focus. So much in my life had gone wrong, so much had been shaken up, that I just wanted some normalcy again … whatever that even meant anymore. Lillian continued to thrive at home; it was I who struggled the most. I didn't know how to cope with everything Lillian had gone through. I felt like I fell short as a mom. I had abandoned Preslee and couldn't fix Lillian. Viewing myself through my own eyes, all I could see was a failure. Returning to work did not serve to make me feel any better about everything else going on in my life.

Lillian had her post-op checkup with her pediatrician a few days after she came home. All of the nurses were ecstatic to see her. They had been following her journey on our Facebook page and were proud of Lillian. My baby was famous at the pediatric office, but sadly it was for all the wrong reasons. Even so, we are very thankful everyone knows and concurs that Lillian is a heart warrior. Her checkup went well, but her doctor was very concerned about her weight. She doesn't like to eat, and even when she does eat she can't gain weight. This is concerning because she registers in the negative for her age category on percentile charts. The pediatrician discussed the possibility of placing an NG

tube again but never went through with it. I was not told
the reason why. Heart babies tend to be on the smaller
side, so our biggest goal now was to help her get bigger
and stronger. She would require surgery to repair her
heart, which we hoped would happen sooner rather than
later, but she needed to weigh more for surgeons to
operate. We continued to fortify her breastmilk with
formula to try to increase her weight.

A couple of days later Jeramy, Preslee, Lillian,
and I were at our friend's house eating barbecue. It felt
good to finally get out of the house and go somewhere. I
was particularly happy to have the chance to spend some
time with our friends. Lillian was due for a diaper
change, so I laid her down on the changing pad and
pulled out a cloth diaper and wet wipes. She was a little
fussy that day, but I didn't think much of it until I
changed her diaper. I unsnapped the buttons and
instantly saw a diaper full of blood. Obviously, this
petrified me. It was a Sunday night, so her pediatric
office was closed. I decided to call the after-hours
exchange. I described Lillian's symptoms and tried to
estimate how much blood was in her diaper. The blood
was mixed in with her bowel movement and smelled like
pennies. The nurse advised us to go to the emergency
room so doctors could examine it. I took only a couple of
bites of my food and then hurried to the hospital. I asked
Jeramy to stay with Preslee at our friend's house because

it was already 7:30 pm, and I didn't know how long we would be in the ER.

When we arrived at the ER, we were taken straight back to an examining room. The doctors came in and watched her closely. They wanted to try to collect some of the poop that had blood in it so they could run some tests. They took a disposable diaper and turned it inside out to create a waterproof surface so that the poop would not soak into the diaper as quickly. Their efforts were unsuccessful, and it ended up being a huge failure.

Lillian finally had a bowel movement and it went everywhere. We were able to save some of it but not enough to send off for a culture. We stayed in that room for what felt like an eternity. I was exhausted, and everyone was clueless as to why she was having bloody stools. The doctor said that it did look as though she had a very small fissure but given the small amount of blood collected there was no way it could be the cause of this problem. They decided to admit her because it was already 1:00 am. I did not want to have to stay, but I was exhausted and wanted to sleep. At this point, I was struggling to keep my eyes open.

We went upstairs to a regular floor: 2 South. This was a floor Lillian had never stayed on before, so I did not feel comfortable with her being assigned to a room on this floor. I previously had been told that because she is a heart baby she would always be admitted to the Transitional Care Unit simply as a precaution. However, they assured me that she would be fine on the main floor because she was not here concerning any problems related to her heart. The nurse who came in started asking me generic questions. Once she found out Lillian was a heart baby, she went into panic mode. She hurried to hook Lillian to a pulse oximeter. She then started drilling me about all of the surgeries she has had and how they normally do not get heart patients on this floor. She did not like hearing that Lillian has had so many issues, and when she found out that she was on ECMO just a couple of weeks ago, I could tell she did not feel comfortable having Lillian as her patient. At this point it was 2 am, and I just wanted to sleep.

The next morning doctors and nurses checked Lillian during their rounds, but this time rounds were so different. I was not familiar with any of these people, and I did not like this at all. I'm used to her being cared for by the Red Team and having the same people attend to her who already know her. I definitely wanted to be in the TCU. They discussed how she had been admitted with bloody stools for unknown reasons. A bunch of second floor training nurse students kept coming in to listen to Lillian's heart. They decided to keep her in the hospital in hopes that they would be able to collect enough poop from her to send off for a culture. We were literally only in the hospital for the purpose of catching poop and scooping it into a container. Everything is always so weird with Lillian, and it seems as though no one can ever figure out what is wrong with her. She is a mysterious baby.

One area on Lillian's right side, where she previously had a drainage line from her last surgery, had a stitch popping out. It was red and looked super irritated. Dr. H and Debbie came up and looked at it to make sure it did not look infected. Then they went ahead and pulled the stitch. They put Betadine on it and covered it with a bandage. They told me to faithfully clean it a couple of times a day and to keep it covered to prevent infection. Lillian was not a fan of having it pulled out, but it looked way less irritated once it was gone. It was so nice to see their familiar faces. Lillian still was not considered one of their patients during this stay, so they asked how she was doing and if we needed anything before they left. It was easy to see they still cared about her.

Two days went by and nothing had changed. Each day at rounds, staff discussed what could be wrong but continued to reiterate how there was no way the blood came from a fissure. On the fourth morning, the doctor came in during rounds and looked at Lillian's bottom. He said, "Oh, look there—a fissure. That must be what is causing her bloody stools. I think we should go ahead and discharge her." It was mind blowing. You have got to be kidding me! Everyone keeps saying they have no idea what is wrong with her but are certain it is not a fissure, and now all of a sudden, I am being told a fissure is the cause of her bleeding. I knew they had no idea what was wrong with her. I didn't care though. I wanted to leave. I was becoming more and more angry at being stuck there with no answers, doing something I could have done at home for her. I gladly packed our bags and waited for the discharge papers.

While waiting, my mom called to tell me Preslee had passed out. She explained that Preslee had been eating pancakes when suddenly she turned pale and fainted. My mom kept trying to wake her up by shaking her and shouting her name, but Preslee remained unresponsive. She was about to call the ambulance when all of a sudden Preslee woke up and the color returned to her face. I could not leave the hospital because they were about to discharge Lillian, so I asked my mom to call Jeramy. They decided to just monitor her because she was not running a fever and started acting completely like herself again. My mom thinks Preslee may have been choking on a pancake. All I could think about was what the heck is happening in my life. I know being a parent can be hard, but I never imagined motherhood would come with so many medical issues and mysteries.

After Lillian was discharged, I picked up Preslee and was glad to see that she was acting completely normal. She was running around and acting like her silly self. I thanked my mom for watching her and headed home. It felt so good to be home, but all I could think about was how long will we get to stay home this time? I knew it would only be a matter of time before we were back at that hospital for something. We still had no idea why Lillian was having bloody stools.

Chapter 17
Waiting for Her Repair

We went to a follow-up appointment with Lillian's cardiologist, Dr. G. This was our first appointment with him since Lillian had been removed from ECMO. Right before she was placed on life support, he called to commend me on how I always know when to seek treatment for Lillian. He said he was very happy to hear that I was so conscientious and attentive to Lillian's incision and oxygen levels. He and I had a long talk that day, and I was delighted that he had called just to stay in the loop. It reassured me that he still cared for Lillian. Now here we are at this appointment, and Dr. G is saying that he cannot believe everything Lillian has gone through and how strange it was when one thing after another kept happening to her. It was a pleasure to finally see him again. He is always so genuine and sweet.

Dr. G listened to Lillian's heart and told her she was a strong baby girl. He asked me how I was doing, and I told him the lie I had been telling to myself and everyone else around me for the past few months—I am fine. This had become my normal response to this question because the truth is too difficult and painful to explain. What I wanted to do was let down my guard and finally tell someone that nothing is fine, that I feel like I'm slowly dying inside, that I am terrified that Lillian will stop breathing when I'm sleeping or at work and I won't be able to save her, that I might possibly have to live my life without Lillian. But instead I smile and tell people I am fine, that I'm just taking it day by day. Dr. G smiled at me and said, "Lillian has been through a lot," almost as if he understood that I was not really okay but would be someday. He asked me if I was still keeping her hooked up to the pulse-ox machine constantly, and I responded that of course I was because I don't trust myself and fear I won't get to her in time if something should happen. He agreed that I had a valid reason to feel scared but said that I was going to drive myself crazy. He again stated his belief that she looked good now, and I should stop using the pulse-ox machine so much, even though he understands why I do.

I told Dr. G that Lillian was having bloody stools. He obviously did not want to hear that. He looked at the pictures I had taken of her bowel movements and agreed that there was too much blood in her stools. He wanted more tests to be run to find an answer to the problem and suggested that we see a gastroenterologist

(GI doctor) to further investigate. He also said that he would like to be informed of the findings. Lillian's 3-month-old check-up was a couple of days later. She was due for her shots. Her pediatrician also wanted answers for the bloody stools, so she called a GI doctor who, fortunately, was able to squeeze us in that day.

He was a pleasant man but didn't seem overly concerned about Lillian's bloody stools. I didn't understand how anyone could think this was normal. He ordered some blood work while wondering if the blood in her stools could be caused by a milk protein allergy. The only problem with that suggestion is that I am lactose intolerant myself, so I do not drink milk. However, the formula we were using to fortify her breast milk could have milk protein in it, so he switched us to Nutramigen to see if that would help. We would still add the same amount of Nutramigen to the breast milk as we had of the other formula so that there would be no crazy change and she would still get the same added calories.

We went into the room where nurses perform the lab work. I explained to the nurse that Lillian was a hard stick, but she was convinced that she could find a vein. I said I would let her try, but only two times and then she would need to quit. She stuck her once and, just as I had anticipated, missed her vein. Lillian was crying at this point, and I hated the way in which I had to hold her. The nurse asked me to hold Lillian's head against my chest. This required me to have to place my hand on her forehead and hold her tight against my chest while holding her other arm straight out. I started to feel sick to my stomach. The room was getting hot and my heart was breaking for Lillian. I never had to hold her during blood draws before, and I am not a fan of needles in the first place. The nurse tried a second time and missed again. This time, instead of stopping, she kept digging the needle around in Lillian's arm. I looked down and watched this lady put the needle in and pull it out of Lillian's arm and felt as though I was going to pass out. I felt like a terrible mother to allow her to torture my daughter like this. I told her she needed to stop.

Another nurse came in, stuck Lillian once, and found a vein. However, because Lillian's veins are so small, which is a common problem in heart patients, the nurse was only able to draw a small amount of blood. I told them that this whole ordeal was too painful for Lillian and I couldn't allow them to draw any more blood. They had gotten all they could get, and we were done. Lillian was exhausted from getting so worked up and fell asleep as soon as I placed her in her car seat. I had so much compassion for her. She had not asked for these problems, and yet it felt like she would never catch a break. If it wasn't one thing, it was another. I wished more than anything that I could take her place.

The weeks went on, and we still had no answers as to why Lillian was having bloody stools. She would go a few days here and there with no blood in her stools when all of sudden she would have a week of nothing but bloody stools. The Nutramigen did not seem to help, so I gave it up. No one had answers, and even though she was having a lot of bloody stools, she was acting fine. I continued to monitor her. Some weeks were better than others. I was happy to be home and to finally start to feel like a mom again, but it was time to get back to my first graders.

When I returned to work, Preslee and Lillian stayed with Maw-Maw during the day. I texted her constantly to check on the girls. I was still struggling to remain focused and decided I needed to talk to my doctor about it. I had lost who I was and was wrestling with my identity. I went into her office and bawled my eyes out. I told her everything that Lillian has been through and admitted how unhappy I was feeling that nothing was going right. She was very sweet and empathetic as she listened to me talk about Lillian. It was a relief for me to finally be able to tell someone that I was not okay.

The doctor diagnosed me with depression and post-traumatic stress disorder (PTSD). She decided to start me on Zoloft, a depression medication, explaining that it should help me concentrate and start to feel better. She did stress, however, that it was not a cure-all and that the past would not go away because of it. I knew in reality that nothing could really fix me, but I so desperately wanted a cure-all. I wanted to put the past behind me and be happy again. I felt like I was suffocating, and to be honest, there were days when I didn't want to live anymore.

The thought of dying kept running through my head. I felt useless in this world. I couldn't fix Lillian. I was failing Preslee by spending so much time away from her. My marriage was rocky. What was the point of living anymore? I was unhappy with my life, and I was tired of feeling this way. I wanted the pain, anxiety, and fear of the unknown to vanish. I was hurting inside, and I was alone. I had become an expert at hiding all of my emotions because I had been doing it for so long. I appeared to have it all together and acted as though I did when in reality I was a phony. I wondered if anyone would miss me and if I even have a purpose in this life. I have heard it said that God never gives someone more than she can handle, which is why he always chooses the strongest women to be heart moms. I treasured this thought because if God hadn't chosen me to be a heart mom, I wouldn't have Lillian. If he had not given me my two beautiful daughters, I might already have ended my life. But any time I thought about committing suicide, my daughters' faces would flash through my mind. I couldn't leave them without a mom. Not only did I need to get professional help, but I also needed to find some type of support.

I found a variety of support groups on Facebook, and some seemed to help, but they also tore me apart. I became obsessed with them. I was constantly reading posts on my phone, and some of them were beneficial. I discovered that I was not the only one who suffered from depression and PTSD, which helped me feel like I wasn't as big of a failure as I saw myself. I started to follow quite a few pages about parents' journeys with their heart warriors. It was refreshing to finally talk to people who could relate to and understand what I was going through. This became a sort of therapy for me, but also triggered some not-so-pleasant memories.

One boy I was following had a more severe congenital heart defect than Lillian. His mom was super sweet, and I frequently prayed for her son. One morning I logged in to the group and discovered that he had passed away suddenly and unexpectedly. I cried during my entire ride to work. Hearing this brought back all the fears I had of Lillian going into cardiac arrest. I wondered if I needed to keep Lillian hooked up to the pulse-ox machine constantly so that if she would go into cardiac arrest, the machine would sound an alarm, and I would be able to save her.

Any time I would come across a post about ECMO, a little fire would spark inside of me, and I would cry. My stomach would get butterflies, and my mind would flash back to August 29, when I thought Lillian wasn't going to make it. Then I would watch as little heart warrior after heart warrior would earn their wings. For a while I had to unfollow these pages because

I couldn't cope with all the deaths. However, I eventually came to appreciate the support I received from these CHD families, recognizing that it was therapeutic for me to have and deal with feelings that arose from posts that triggered me. I was finally starting to accept that it was okay to not be okay. So many families are traveling on the same journey as I am, and I was so thankful to everyone who shared their stories.

I learned about a program called Beads of Courage. Our hospital does not participate in the program, so we signed Lillian up for the beads through the mail program. This program was designed to give children a visual representation of their bravery and strength. The program is for cardiac, burn, and cancer patients, along with a few others. Lillian has been through so much in her short life so far, and I wanted her to see how strong and brave she really was through all her trials. The program gives hope and strength not only to the children but to their families as well. Enrollment was pretty easy, and I received her beads within a few weeks. It was difficult to backtrack all she has been through, so I did the best I could. Each bead represents a treatment, needle poke, echocardiogram, X-ray, respiratory support, heart surgery, general surgery, and so much more. Lillian had over four hundred beads that we needed to catch up on. The yellow beads represent days in the hospital. The pink ones are for respiratory support, the black for IV/needle pokes, and the silver heart corresponds to heart surgery. The echocardiogram bead glows in the dark, and the round clay bead signifies each day on ECMO. The list goes on and on. Beads might designate a special milestone, transitioning from one unit to the next, having physical therapy, displaying courage, or experiencing family firsts. If a child has gone through it, there's a bead for it.

When I received Lillian's beads in the mail, I was so emotional. They had given her a wooden box in the shape of a puppy dog to keep her beads in, a colorful bag decorated with cats to hold the strands, and lots of beads in many different colors. I worked for hours to string each bead onto the necklace. As I stranded each one, it brought back the painful reality of the past four months. I started the strand by spelling out her name and continued to strand bead by beautiful bead. Yellow, glow in the dark, black, orange, white, yellow ... I continued for hours and hours until I had finally placed her last hard-earned bead. Stranding made for good therapy.

After it was completed, I admired it and sighed. The strand was so long, but it was breathtaking to look at it and realize how much Lillian has gone through. One day she will look at her beads, realize everything she has been through, and appreciate how she has never had to fight this battle alone. She will understand how strong and brave she was during each and every trial.

I look forward to receiving more beads. Stranding beads was my therapy. It kept me going. Each time I strand another bead to her necklace, it breaks me a little more because it is another challenge and obstacle Lillian has had to overcome, but at the same time, it pulls me back together because I can smile knowing Lillian is still here and still fighting. Beads of courage shined a light on my dark world. I pray that when Lillian is feeling down and things don't seem to be going the way she plans, she can look at her beads and continue to let them shine light on her as they do for me. I hung her beads in her bedroom, knowing that there would be more to come. Every time I walk into her room, I see them, and they remind me to be thankful for the life I am living with her.

My brother, his fiancé, and her family arranged an event to raise money for Lillian. They created a beer pong tournament at her workplace. Her family loves to grill, and they do it as a hobby. Their food is delicious, and they make the best barbecue I have ever eaten. We went to the tournament and were surprised to see so many people there. We were truly blessed and thankful to see so many people come and support my sweet baby girl. They raised a substantial amount of money to help pay for Lillian's medical bills and to cover the many days and weeks that I had to take off work without pay. Things like this are what kept me going. Being surrounded by generous, loving people reminded me to be grateful when I was feeling down.

As the weeks and months went by, I would sometimes forget that Lillian had a broken heart. It was fun to dress her up as an old lady for Halloween and go trick or treating with Preslee, the Rainbow Fish. It was rejuvenating to finally start to engage in some life activities again like a normal mom. Other than the bloody stools, Lillian was doing well. Thanksgiving rolled around, and I found it enjoyable to spend another holiday and month at home with Lillian. I was still missing a lot of work for doctor appointments and follow-ups for Lillian. This put a drain on our finances because I had to take a lot of unpaid days off work. When our financial burden started to rear its ugly head, there was nothing I could do about it because I had to take care of Lillian regardless of the cost. There were bills that needed to be paid now, and Lillian's hospital bills were continuing to roll in. I definitely had my good days and my bad ones, but thank God I was finally enjoying more good days than bad.

Lillian had a follow-up appointment with Dr. G. He announced that she was ready for her full heart repair, but she needed to gain some weight first. She was not quite eleven pounds, and he wouldn't feel comfortable performing the surgical repair unless she weighed at least twelve pounds. This was discouraging to hear because we had tried everything to get her to gain weight, but she just would not eat well. I tried feeding her baby food, but she hated it, so that obviously wasn't going to put any weight on her. My primary goal was to get her to eat more, and I tried to do this the best I could.

Christmas was around the corner, which meant Lillian's heart was probably going to be repaired soon. She had a follow-up appointment with Dr. G, and she was just shy of twelve pounds. He decided to go ahead and proceed with the surgery because her oxygen saturation was in the low seventies. I was nervous, but it honestly didn't hit me until someone from the hospital called to set up a date and time for the operation. My heart fell into my stomach when I received that call. All of the fears that I thought I had dealt with came flooding back at full force. We decided to schedule her surgery on December 28 because I would be on winter break from school, and I really couldn't afford to miss any more work. I even had an ornament made for her first Christmas. It was shaped like a heart and had a Band-Aid on it, along with an engraving of her name and surgery dates.

Thank God I work for an amazing school district in such a compassionate community. They were all aware of my family's struggles and have displayed a love for Lillian. They did everything they could do to help my family during these difficult times. Right before winter break I was informed that the middle school students were working on a project to help raise money for my family to pay for Lillian's hospital bills and the expenses we incurred from me missing work and traveling to and from the hospital.

The students worked on a service learning project in which they came up with ideas to help my family. Each advisory conducted research to learn more about Tetralogy of Fallot with Pulmonary Atresia. They looked up the definition, treatment options, methods and surgeries available to "fix" her heart, and the struggles a family may face in raising a child who suffers from this illness. Then each advisory had to come up with an idea to raise money for my family. My principal asked if I would bring the girls to school so that the students could present me with the money they had raised, along with a few gifts.

When I arrived at school with my girls, we were given a few greeting cards with visa money cards inside. The students had included some very sweet messages and letters in the cards. They had raised a significant amount of money to help us with Lillian's hospital bills and other expenses. They also gave us a gift basket with toys, candy, and snacks for Preslee. A *Farmington Press* reporter covered the event and wrote an article for the newspaper. Our story made the front cover. This was icing on the cake because it helped to spread awareness of CHD. I could not believe that the students had planned every detail, even thinking to give Preslee a gift. They also made Love necklaces and ornaments on the 3D printer at school.

I have never felt prouder to work somewhere before. I knew God had placed me at this school in this community for a reason, and I could never be more thankful. Everyone has been very supportive of my family and of my having to miss so many days of work. They truly helped me during my weakest times and gave me less to stress about. That morning I went to the middle school to look at the posters the students had made about Lillian. It was awesome to see the hard work and dedication they showed in learning about my baby girl and her special heart. My heart was warm and content. I was at peace, and their generosity and posters brought me to tears. What an honor it is to work in such a loving and caring community.

Winter break at work finally arrived. I spent the first couple of days running around like a chicken with my head cut off. There was so much I needed to accomplish before Lillian's heart repair, not to mention we had multiple Christmas family events to attend. I tried my best to keep Lillian away from any germs. We could not let her get sick; otherwise her surgery would be postponed. As badly as I wanted it to be postponed, I knew it had to happen eventually, and I wanted it to be over.

On Christmas morning, we woke the girls up and they opened their gifts. It was a very peaceful morning. Seeing Preslee's face light up when she opened her gifts filled my heart with joy. She would show Lillian each gift as she opened it, and Lillian would start laughing. After opening gifts, we headed to my parents' house to celebrate Christmas with them. Preslee was so excited to see her cousins. We had a pretty lazy day and eventually headed home to sleep. We were now three days away from Lillian's surgery.

I woke up the next morning, and my stomach was hurting. I thought maybe I had to use the restroom, so I did. Then my mouth felt like it had a weird taste. I was convinced something was not right. Before I knew it, I was praying to the porcelain god (throwing up) in the toilet. I had caught a stomach bug and it was bad. Jeramy was already at work, so I was home alone with both girls. This day was not going to go well. Lillian had a neurology appointment and also had to meet with her heart surgeon for a pre-operation appointment. I called my mom and begged her to come get the girls. I could not stop throwing up. The room was spinning, and I felt like death. I could not leave the bathroom without having to turn around and run right back to the toilet. Preslee kept crying for me, and Lillian needed to be fed. Oh, how I could so not do this.

My mom luckily showed up just in time. She packed the bags for the girls and loaded them and the girls in the car. I already knew Lillian would most likely miss her neurology appointment, but I didn't want her to miss her pre-op. As soon as my mom left with the girls, my phone rang. It was the surgeon's office calling to let me know that they needed to move Lillian's surgery up one day. It would now take place tomorrow instead of in two days. This was awful. I was as sick as a dog and I had to get better. There is no way I could miss her surgery. I was also praying that she would not get sick. This surgery had to happen; I had to get better—and quick! The heart surgeon's office cancelled Lillian's appointment and said that they would discuss the surgery in the morning. We needed to arrive at 7 am; surgery would start at 9 am.

I called Jeramy to let him know. He decided to leave work because I needed help with the girls. He was going to see if the heart surgeon could get Lillian in for her pre-op that day and also see if neurology could squeeze her in for the appointment we had missed. Everything was happening so fast. Then my mom called. On the way to the city for appointments, Preslee had started throwing up. This was a nightmare! My mom had to bring Preslee back to me because we needed to keep her and Lillian separated. Preslee and I cuddled all day. She practically slept her sickness away, while I couldn't keep any food down. I was still feeling terrible, and Lillian's surgery was quickly approaching.

Chapter 18
Her Heart Is Repaired

Jeramy and I agreed that Preslee and I needed to stay away from Lillian because we were sick. The hospital is over an hour away from our house, so we decided that Preslee and I would stay in a hotel while he and Lillian stayed at my parents' house. I was still feeling awful, but I checked into our hotel room and Preslee and I were able to quickly fall asleep. I woke up the next morning, still not feeling the best, but at least I was not throwing up anymore. Preslee also seemed to be feeling better. We went downstairs to get breakfast. I could not eat anything, but Preslee was able to eat one plain donut. Jeramy picked us up from the hotel, and we dropped Preslee off at my sister's house because we didn't want her at the hospital, especially since she wasn't feeling well.

When we arrived at the hospital, we went upstairs to surgery registration. A lady called me back into a room and asked me a few questions about Lillian to get her registered. I was still feeling pretty cruddy and was struggling to focus. We were all wearing our "Love for Lillian" shirts. We asked everyone to wear their shirt today to support Lillian. Her footprints from when she was on ECMO were pictured on the front of the shirt. Many people bought shirts and were wearing them to support Lillian! It was astonishing to see her Facebook page filled with pictures of people from everywhere who were thinking about her and praying for her. We went back into the pre-op area. I wore a yellow mask because I wanted to see Lillian before they took her back to surgery. I held her in my arms while answering a few more questions and talking to the anesthesiologist. This was the first time that Lillian was having a planned surgery, and I was scared.

I had too much time to think about this surgery. I also was not feeling well, and because they had canceled Lillian's pre-op appointment, I felt very unprepared. Dr. H came in and started to explain what would be happening in the operating room. As I have mentioned before, he is a very quiet man. He does not say much but cuts straight to the point. He said that they would get her all hooked up first, and then they would start the procedure.

The plan was to place her on bypass. This means that her heart would purposely be stopped so they could do the repair without her heart beating. They would go in and fix her ventricular septal defect (VSD) so that there would no longer be a hole separating her ventricles. Then they would place a conduit, which is a device to extend her pulmonary artery so that an adequate amount of blood flow can go to each lung. They would also remove both of her BT shunts. Then they would take her off of bypass to see if her heart would start beating again. They would place temporary pacemaker wires so that if she needed a pacemaker, they would be able to hook her up immediately. This was the first time we heard mention of the pacemaker, and it terrified me to hear those words. It made me think of an elderly person. Of course, Jeramy had questions about this too.

I was too sick to even think. There was obviously a lot more to this procedure than he had explained, or that I could even understand, but I trusted this man. He has proven time and time again that we picked the best surgeon to repair Lillian's heart. We gave her our kisses, but I didn't want to let her go. I was terrified. I said a quick prayer and kissed her through my yellow mask. I looked in Lillian's eyes and reminded her that she is very brave and very strong. I told her that I loved her more than she would ever know, kissed her little hands, and handed her over to the nurse.

I watched them walk down the hall holding Lillian. I felt so guilty that she had no idea what was about to happen. Then we went to the private waiting room and waited for surgery to call. I was a nervous wreck. My mom, Maw-Maw, and Jeramy were there the entire time. Lillian was taken back to surgery early, at 8 am. At 11:05 am, they called to tell me that her lines were a little hard to place, but they were finally able to get them in and surgery was starting. At 12:40 pm, Lillian was placed on bypass; her heart was purposely stopped. This was the most heart-wrenching call. It is terrifying to hear that your almost seven-month-old daughter's heart is stopped. I had flashbacks to August 29, the day they had placed her on life support. Every inch of my body was filled with fear. I waited impatiently until I got the next call. At 1:35 pm Lillian's VSD was completely closed. The surgeon explained that from the looks of it, she may require the pacemaker. Her VSD was bigger than he had anticipated, but only time would tell. At 2:50 pm, Lillian was off bypass and surgeons were closing her up. She did well, and they believed she would not need the pacemaker after all because her heart seemed to be beating in rhythm. This was magnificent news.

All day I struggled to stay awake. I was still trying to fight off this sickness. I felt like a terrible mom, as I was actually able to sleep somewhat. My daughter was back in surgery, and here I was sleeping. I couldn't help it though. I was weak, lightheaded, and felt like death. At 3:45 pm, Dr. H came in and said Lillian had done well. Her arteries look good, and currently, she doesn't require the pacemaker. They planned to move her to the PICU shortly, and we would be able to see her around 5 pm. The good news was that Lillian probably would not need another surgery until she is around five years old, because the surgeons were able to place a larger conduit in her. As long as it does not shrink, which does happen sometimes, we may finally get a break from this crazy journey.

We were finally able to go to her room to see her. When we asked what room she was in, they said, "Room 2508." Wait! Did they just say room 2508? NOPE! I don't want this room. This is not a good room. This is a bad room full of bad memories. As I walked toward the door, my heart was pounding. This was the room in which Lillian had coded, the room in which Lillian almost died, the room in which I spent the worst days of my life. Lillian had been on ECMO in this room, fighting for her life.

All I could imagine was the chaos that had gone on in that room just a few months before. I could see the door that once was decorated with pictures of Lillian, the door that had Lillian's name displayed at the top with pink and purple bows and decorations covering it. I looked over and could once again feel the chilling feeling I had gotten the day I saw Lillian lying there, practically dead. In my mind I could see the blood still splattered on the floor. I could see the baby doll that had been thrown under the laundry bin amidst the chaos and see her little pink and white owl sock missing from her foot. I could see my daughter lying there connected to the many machines in her room that held the keys to her life. The room had felt full that day, with so many doctors and nurses surrounding her. This is a room that is normally bright and colorful, but in my mind, it looks black and white. My heart was hurting as I walked through the door of room 2508. This room is forever ruined for me, and I don't want to be in it.

When I walked in the room and looked at Lillian, I was relieved to see that she was okay. It never gets easier seeing your baby hooked to a bunch of machines. She was bleeding around her incision more than they would like, and they were monitoring her red urine. She had a hematoma on her neck caused by surgeons trying to put in an arterial line. It was sad to see the big blue knot on her neck. I was told that it should go down on its own over time.

The surgeon also informed us that he had to give her blood in the operating room. She looked so bruised and swollen. She was still intubated and medically paralyzed. Her eyes were puffy, and she looked as though she had gained a lot of weight. Again, this baby did not look like my beautiful Lillian. But I knew in time she would get better and look like herself again. I hate more than anything that she has to go through this. I hate that any baby does, but especially my baby. I get very emotional going through this with her. It has brought back a lot of bad memories that I have worked so hard to bury deep inside. All of the emotions flooded back into my body again, and I couldn't control my feelings of sadness and anger. But I was also thankful that she had made it through another surgery and her heart was beating again.

Some of our favorite PICU nurses came in to visit Lillian. They kept talking about how beautiful she is and how much she has grown. Nurses who weren't even assigned to Lillian for the day came in just to say hi. This is the place that had become our second home. We have created a family here full of amazing, talented nurses and doctors. Although we still have some of the worst memories from here, they have all led to good memories because Lillian is alive. It was so good to see familiar faces who remembered Lillian and loved her like their own child. Even though I did not like this room, I did like the nurses and couldn't help but imagine a happy ending to all of this.

Lillian did well on the first day. The next morning, they decided to start weaning her off her pain medicine. She was a little uncomfortable when she started to wake up. She had developed a little fluid on the right side of her chest and a thick yucky cough. Her oxygen levels had dropped to 81 percent that day when she was not on oxygen, so they placed her on 1 liter of oxygen to help her out. She remained pretty out of it that day but fortunately was able to be extubated. Her red urine stopped, so they also took her Foley (catheter) out. She was taking very small baby steps, but it was still progress. She was even able to eat if she acted hungry, which was encouraging considering she hadn't eaten in two days.

On the third day, she seemed to be doing okay. Nurses were able to wean her off the fentanyl and were rotating pain medications so that she would not have to stay on narcotics long. She had a couple of doses of oxycodone to help when absolutely necessary, but Tylenol seemed to help quite a bit, so she didn't really need the harder stuff. She was very sleepy but her urine output was not very good, so they upped her Lasix. Both of her IVs went out, so transportation services had to come to her room to poke her again. It made me so sad to hear this because Lillian is a hard stick. I was counting her bruises and needle holes earlier in the day and counted over twenty-eight pokes that they had made on her tiny little body.

The nurses kept trying to wean Lillian off oxygen all day, but her oxygen levels would instantly drop into the low 80s as soon as she was off the oxygen. She still had a lot of fluid showing up on her right side in X- rays, and her liver looked to be swollen. Doctors said that this was normal. They started to monitor the right side of her heart closely and decided to increase her heart medication because her heart was working too hard. Her heart rate was staying in the 170s when resting and going over the 200s when angry. Her goal heart rate is 100-125, so they absolutely did not like seeing it so high.

I got to hold Lillian for the first time since her repair that night while the nurse changed her bedding. When I picked her up, she instantly stopped crying and looked very content, which made my heart so happy. While I was holding Lillian, alarms started going off in the PICU. There was a code blue. All of the nurses and doctors started running to the code room. It was two doors down: Room 2505. The PICU seemed like a ghost town. Then I saw them wheel in the ECMO machine. Chills ran down my spine because I now knew exactly what it must have been like the day Lillian went on ECMO. Sadly, I had been at work, so I did not witness this happen to her, but it was described to me in messages shortly after Lillian was placed on ECMO.

I could now fully see the chaos that had gone on that day. Lillian's surgery had to be moved up because there was a heart baby born who really needed the surgeon's time that had been scheduled for Lillian. I had a feeling this was that baby. I will never know, but I prayed so hard for that baby. I felt sick to my stomach, and all of my old fears came flooding back into my body. I cried when I looked at Lillian. I was so thankful she had survived, because sadly, a lot of patients do not. That baby was so tiny. I would see her as I walked past her room to go get something to eat. Her tiny little body was lying on the bed hooked to all of those big scary machines. Each time I passed her room, I would pray for her.

Recovery was pretty rough for Lillian this time. She had a terrible cough, so someone from respiratory had to come up and work with her. He would take this little pink tool and beat it on her side, which I could sympathetically feel on my side, but I knew it needed to be done to get the gunk out. It was so hard to see Lillian in so much pain. She would look at me with the most pitiful face and glossy eyes each time she would cough. I broke down that day and questioned the world. Why did this have to happen to Lillian? Why did she have to have a broken heart? Why does she have to be in pain? It didn't seem fair.

Most days I was able to hide my fears and be strong for Lillian, but I've been falling apart for months now. After rounds, I went downstairs to the cafeteria to get something to eat for breakfast. While I was gone, doctors decided to pull her pacemaker wires and central line. However, there was a big miscommunication, which should not have happened. They were supposed to give her a dose of fentanyl before pulling her lines because the process can be very painful, and they wanted her to be able to relax.

When I walked back in the room, Lillian was screaming. Big alligator tears were rolling down her cheeks. The nurse said she had never received the orders to give her pain medicine, and when she walked in the room, Dr. H was already pulling her lines out. She said she had no idea that he was going to pull them out yet and was shocked when she came in the room to see they had just been pulled out. Lillian was screaming, and I could tell she was in pain. The nurse went ahead and gave Lillian the dose of pain medicine after the fact, which seemed to help. This was a horrific mistake that should not have happened. Other than that, she was doing pretty well and was able to go to the TCU.

While sitting in the hospital, I had a lot of time to keep track of each bead Lillian would need so I could add them to her strand. I didn't want to miss a single one because they are so important to documenting her journey. This project helped to keep my mind busy during this chaotic hospital stay. It also helped to remind me that my daughter is brave and strong. When she was fussy and crying in pain and discomfort, I would look to these beads for comfort, as each represented something that had already taken place that she hopefully wouldn't have to go through again. It kills me as her mother to not be able to take her pain away. I am thankful that she will have these beads to look back on one day. It was my goal to keep track of which beads she needed and to not forget a single one. I wanted her beads to tell her story as close to reality as possible, so she can tell her own story one day through her beads. Lillian is my hero and the strongest person I have ever met, and I don't want her to ever forget that.

We spent Lillian's first New Year's Eve at the hospital, which was also her seven-month birthday. I brought a cute little dress for her to wear. Daddy brought Preslee to the hospital so that we could all celebrate together. It is so crazy to be living this life. Most of our friends were out celebrating the holiday—all dressed up, going to fun places, and celebrating with friends and family—but we were here at the hospital in a very small TCU room. There really wasn't much going on. Preslee was tired and crabby. It really is not a fun place for anyone to be, especially a toddler. We called it a night early and Preslee and Daddy went home.

It was Lillian's seven-month birthday, so I took her milestone picture in a hospital bed. It was crazy to think that I was yet again taking her monthly picture at a hospital instead of at home. The last time I took a monthly picture at the hospital was at three months old, when she was on ECMO and about to be wheeled back to the operating room to get a new BT Shunt. I never imagined that I would be celebrating a holiday in the hospital, but this is what life was for us now. I am a heart mom, and all that matters to me is my children's health. I would spend every holiday at the hospital if I had to, as long as it meant Lillian wouldn't have to be alone.

Lillian had to get an NG tube placed and was not able to stay off of oxygen long. She was not eating much, and when she did, she would spit it all up. Any time she would fall asleep, her oxygen would drop down into the 80s. Thankfully, each X-ray was showing progress, so we were heading in the right direction.

Lillian just needed more time to recover. We spent the next couple of days trying to keep her off of oxygen and getting her to eat more.

I found out that Lillian's VSD was about 22 mm. That is such a huge hole in such a tiny heart. Imagine a hole a little larger than half an inch inside a walnut! That's a crazy image! These heart surgeons perform surgery on such teeny tiny hearts. It really does amaze me when I think about this and try to put it into perspective.

I received the donor card that showed Lillian received donor tissue for her aortic valve and conduit. It was like a reality slap. It made me so sad to think that someone had to die to save Lillian's life. They gave Lillian a gift that wouldn't have been possible without donors. I decided to reach out to the organization to let them know to whom the donor tissue had gone.

I explained Lillian's story and expressed my gratitude to whoever was the donor. It was a real wakeup call to count my blessings and to be thankful. The lady wrote me back to say she was inspired by Lillian and would pass on our information if the family chose to know who had received the tissue. I wrote a note to them, telling them who I was. I mentioned Lillian's past and all she had been through. I told them that I did not know who they are or what their story was that had led to the donation, but I prayed that they would find comfort in knowing that by donating tissue, they had saved Lillian's life. I included pictures of Lillian with my letter.

We were able to go on a wagon ride for the first time ever with Lillian as an inpatient. They wanted to get her moving to help break up the gunk in her chest and to see if the wagon ride would help her any. The doctor put in orders to encourage me to take her out in the wagon around the TCU floor. I was excited to be able to walk out of the room with her, but I was nervous too. I was always told that there are so many sicknesses in the hospital that would not be good for Lillian to catch, so the last thing I wanted to do was venture out in the halls where she could be exposed to those germs. But the doctors thought it would be a good idea, so I did. I had Preslee with me for one of the rides we went on during the next couple of days, and she really enjoyed riding around in a wagon for the first time ever with her sissy.

The next day, Lillian was able to stay off of oxygen and was also able to lose her NG tube, as she was finally keeping all of her feedings down. She was discharged after only a nine-day stay in the hospital. She would have been discharged even sooner if she had not required oxygen. It was such a relief to me that my daughter's heart was finally repaired.

Walking out of that hospital was emotional. I didn't know when I would next see the Red Team or the amazing nurses. I couldn't help but reflect on the past seven months. I cannot believe that so much time has come and gone already. Lillian has been through so much. She shouldn't have to see any of these nice people for a few years, if not more. It was bittersweet. I was happy to leave but was sad because this has been our life for the past seven months. The hospital has been our home away from home. I was thrilled to be heading home with Lillian though. It was finally time to be a normal family and get to stay home for a while. Lillian could start to learn what it is like to be home and be part of a family.

Chapter 19
New Problems Will Always Arise

I was so relieved to finally be home. Having all of us under the same roof is always a secure feeling. I was able to go back to work while my awesome Maw-Maw took care of both of my daughters during the day. In a way, life finally seemed to slow down. It was such a satisfying feeling. Lillian has the heart of a warrior; God designed her to survive! I could not be prouder to be her mommy. On days like today, I look back at Lillian's journey and am inspired by her, a seven-month-old baby girl. She has gone through so much in her short life, more than most people go through in their entire lives. I am excited that we are quickly approaching the time when we will finally get a break from all of these heart surgeries so Lillian can fully recover and just enjoy being a baby! There's nowhere to go from here but up!

December 27 is Lillian's heartiversary, and we plan to celebrate it each year. She is stronger than I am or ever could be. I pray that one day she will look back at her scars and remember that each one tells the most incredible, unspoken story of survival. I promise to spend every waking moment building up her confidence and teaching her to love her scars and her past as much as I love her with or without scars, notwithstanding her past. She is gorgeous, brave, and courageous, and her smile lights up my world. I love her more than she will ever know! Anyone who comes into her life is lucky to get a piece of her. I pray that she never questions her self-worth because God created her for a purpose, knowing everything she would have to endure to fulfill it, and he has big things in store for her!

I was getting ready for Lillian's post-op appointment and couldn't help but think about all of the love and support my family has been shown throughout these past seven months. I wanted to make other people's day and let them know that we heart mamas always stick together. With CHD month coming up in February, I decided to make "Mama to a Heart Warrior" water bottles and little stuffed monkeys with hearts on their chest. I dropped them off to the PICU at Lillian's appointment. We sat in the waiting room, and this time I felt at peace. I can't do much for others because Lillian's hospital bills have kept us on a tight budget lately, but throughout this journey I have learned that the small things are what really matter, just knowing that someone cares about you and your heart baby enough to send a small gift.

Lillian's name was finally called. An X-Ray was taken and the results were good. Dr. H came in and examined her. He said that she was healing nicely and we could stop covering her incision. Her heart rate was still higher than he would have liked, but he thought that it may be normal for her. She has always had a high heart rate, so he wasn't overly concerned. I couldn't help but get emotional. I was staring at the man who has saved my daughter's life multiple times. He is the reason why Lillian is still alive. He has literally held her heart in his hands. He has stopped her heart and made it beat again. He has cut through her chest multiple times to repair her heart. I owe my life to this man, but I have no words to sincerely express my appreciation and love for him.

Dr. H saves lives every single day, and I have seen him sacrifice his own life to save others. He practically lives at the hospital and has devoted his life to pediatric heart patients. I asked him if I could take a picture of him with Lillian because we had been praying and expecting that she would not see him for a long time. When he held her close to his heart, my heart melted to see the affection in the way the two of them looked at each other. Lillian was smiling at him as if she intuitively knew that he was the reason she was still breathing. It has been said that a picture paints a thousand words. My picture of Dr. H and Lillian paints a thousand billion words, and I will treasure it forever.

Each person at the hospital has been extraordinarily good to my family. I was super emotional but greatly relieved to walk out of that hospital with my baby.

Bringing Lillian home was exhilarating. Her appointment went well, and we were waiting for her next follow-up appointment with her cardiologist. I could tell that her breathing was beginning to become labored. She was acting fine, but I could see how hard it was for her to breathe. I continued to monitor her oxygen levels, which were in the 91-96 range. These are excellent numbers compared to what we are used to seeing with Lillian. She also had not had a bloody stool in the past two days, since before her surgery. It was gratifying to feel like she was finally going to get a break from all of the medical drama. She will no longer be glued to a bed and, at eight months old now, will finally have the opportunity to start reaching age milestones. She is developmentally behind, which I have been told is normal for heart patients. Sadly, all she can do now is hold her head up.

Lillian finally had her follow-up appointment. I was praying for good news but had a weird feeling that something was wrong. Her labored breathing gave me a gut feeling that I wouldn't receive good news. We were here for an echocardiogram. I had made Lillian a shirt that says, "My cardiologist beats yours." Everyone in the office thought it was adorable. I also made Preslee a lab coat that says, "Dr. Wilson, cardiologist in training."

Preslee has no choice but to go to all of Lillian's appointments with me, and she is such a trooper about it. She always wants to listen to my heart and Sissy's, so I knew this would be perfect for her. She walked around that office like she was the cutest girl on the planet, which she is in my unbiased opinion. Everyone adored her and loved her outfit.

During the echo, the technician became a little quiet. Lillian was getting fussy, and I was doing everything in my power to make her happy. If you are a heart mom, you can totally relate. Getting a baby, or even a small child, to sit still long enough for a procedure like this and not cry (you or the baby) is hard work and is nearly impossible. When Lillian cries, her blood flow appears as splatters on the screen, making it difficult for the technician to get a good view of her heart. She kept trying to reposition the throb on Lillian's chest to obtain a better view, but I could tell that she was struggling to see the blood flow. Lillian would go through fazes in which she was fine and then would start crying again.

We tried giving Lillian sweeties, which most babies love. It is pretty much just sugar water. Ever since Lillian was a newborn, she had to be given sweeties whenever an echo or any other test was performed to help keep her calm or to distract her. We jokingly called them her REESE'S Peanut Butter Cups. This occasionally did the trick in the past, but she was older now and was starting to catch on. Now it would work only for a couple of seconds. The technician was finally able to get most of the views she needed of Lillian's heart but said that she was having difficulty seeing particular parts, so she wanted the cardiologist to take a look at it. I knew from past experience that this was code for "something is not right, but I need the cardiologist to confirm it."

Dr. G came in the room and explained to me that the technician was struggling to see Lillian's pulmonary artery passing adequate blood flow. He said that during her last surgery, her heart surgeon had informed him that her right pulmonary artery branch was narrow, so he had to balloon it. I had no idea what this meant, but Dr. G assured me that it was not a huge deal and I shouldn't panic. After he performed the echo, he said that there was a small problem but assured me that he would explain more about it when we returned to the examining room. I picked Lillian up off the table and carried her back to room one.

Dr. G explained that Lillian's right pulmonary artery branch is already narrowing. This means that an adequate amount of blood is not getting to her lungs, which is not only bad for the heart but also for the lungs. She is too small for a stent to be placed. The plan is for us to return in three months, at which time he will listen to her lungs and perform another echo. He tried to prepare me for the worst, saying that he was pretty sure

Lillian was not getting an adequate amount of blood flow to each lung, and the problem is significant enough that it requires intervention. In three months, if it does not look any better, she will have to have a bronchoscopy (a test to examine the airways) performed to test her blood flow to each lung. Depending on the results, she will require a cardiac cath to balloon her pulmonary artery again. Because she is too small for a stent, she will need to have periodic bronchs, as her pulmonary artery narrows, until she is big enough to have the permanent stent placed.

Although this was not the worst news he could have given me, it also was not the best. I had been looking forward to Lillian finally getting a break and not needing more surgeries for a while, as well as not having to always be on the go and worry so much. This was not going to happen now. Lillian has always been a rule breaker, so I should have known better. She fooled me big time. It was such a bummer to once again receive news that was not in Lillian's favor. But I am a heart mom who has learned to lean on other heart moms and reach out for prayers and support in my time of need, as well as to pray for and support other moms when they need me. I have learned that things never go as planned. Perhaps most important, I have learned that I am a stronger person because of Lillian, and I appreciate life so much more now. I still have days when I am depressed, but I also have many happy days. I now prepare myself for the worst but always hope for the best. All I know is I am so thankful to have Lillian in my life.

I scheduled Lillian's appointment with the cardiologist for three months out. In April, she will go back to him so he can see where she stands from a cardiac standpoint. She went to a follow-up appointment with neurology to address her seizures and brain bleeds from ECMO. The appointment went well, but it could have gone better. The neurologist looked at Lillian and mentioned that she was pretty far behind in her milestones but was happy to hear that she has been receiving occupational therapy. He confirmed that the EEG taken when she had her seizures did show seizure activity and decided to keep her on the Keppra for another three months.

In three months, we will have another EEG performed and then a follow-up appointment after the EEG to discuss the results and the possibility of taking Lillian off of Keppra. It would be comforting to me for her to be taken off the Keppra, but I am afraid that she will have more seizures if she isn't taking the medicine. Watching her have to be bagged in order to breathe again was terrifying enough, but the thought that this could happen again, only this time at home, did not help to put me at ease. I didn't want to have to chance this happening to her at home with only me there to perform CPR.

Chapter 20
Love for Logan

I rushed out to the mailbox one morning, hoping to see that some dresses I had ordered for Preslee and Lillian for Easter had been delivered. Both girls were still sleeping, so it was the perfect time for me to slip out of the house. It was cold and rainy, so I put on my tennis shoes, ran to the mailbox, grabbed the letters and packages, and hurried back inside. I sat on the living room floor and looked at a couple of the packages and could tell by the return address on one of them that it was the Easter dresses. There was also an envelope addressed to me that did not include a return address. This struck me as odd, so I opened it up and a few pictures fell onto the floor.

My first thought was, who is this gorgeous boy? Wow, he is a handsome little guy. I sat there and admired the pictures for quite some time, and then I read the note:

First of all, we just wanted to let you know that we think Lillian is beautiful. We are so glad that she could be blessed through Logan to receive what she needed, and we are praying for her full recovery and good health.

Logan was a typical boy in many ways. He loved to climb, jump, dance, laugh and play. He loved anything and everything that had to do with being outdoors or on the family farm. He loved Spider-Man, Blue Tractor videos, animals, music, his sticker book, wearing everyone else's shoes, climbs up everything without fear, cuddling with his star blankie, dancing his super cute dance moves, and "not catching" fish (even though he caught them). He gave amazing hugs and kisses to all. Logan loved playing with and teasing his sister Kendra. He was energetic, loving and trusting of everyone. He also loved family sandwich hugs and mowing with the men. Logan exemplified his great love for Christ. He would even pray out loud at bedtime and before meals with us. Some famous Logan quotes are: "I do it, do it again, I pray, what else?, best boat, biscuit gravy yogurt, I ride baby tractor, I go to show, I work with daddy and grandpa, excavator," and yelling, "Mommy's home!"

So about us. I (Lisa) teach fourth grade at a Christian school. My husband Drew is a crop farmer. We have a 5-year-old daughter named Kendra who will soon be 6.

Our son loved being on our family farm with his daddy and his grandpa; he wanted to be there every moment he could. Whenever we left to take him to daycare, Logan would cry and say, "I work with daddy. I ride in baby tractor. I go to shop." My husband and I eventually decided to pull the kids from daycare and let them go to work with daddy and grandpa instead. Since Drew grew up on the farm with his dad, passing this on to our children was important.

On August 17, 2017, it was at the end of the school day when my cell phone rang. I heard that Logan rolled his neck up in the car window while at work with his daddy and grandpa. They brought him back by doing CPR, but he was on a ventilator and had an extensive brain injury. With a severe injury like this, while we were all praying for a miraculous recovery, his organs continued to shut down. We knew we wanted to be able to help other families if we could, so we asked if Logan was a candidate for organ donation if things came to that. After a week-long fight in the hospital, Logan passed away on 8/24/17 with over 20 friends and family members in his hospital room singing praise and worship songs.

While Logan was in the hospital, my friend started a prayer and support page for Logan where I could easily update family and friends. Through that, our church, and our community, there has been a huge outpouring of love and support from family, friends, and even strangers, both during the week of Logan's accident and into the present time as well. We have heard of many people who have come to Christ through Logan and his accident. While that provides some comfort, God is the main reason we can truly get through this tragedy. Receiving your letter and hearing from you that Logan was able to possibly save another child's life, not only warms our hearts but also provides additional comfort to us as it furthers his story and his impact on others.

Since this situation is new to us, we just want you to know that we are open to as much or as little communication as you would like. If you want to stay in touch, we can continue to communicate through the Indiana Donor Network. However, if it ever seems easier to call, email, or send correspondence directly to us, then we give the Indiana Donor Network permission to share our personal contact information with you. Either way, please feel free to ask any questions that you have about Logan or our family, as well as sharing as much or as little as you want about your family and Lillian.

We have enclosed several pictures for you. Two of the pictures are of Drew and my personal favorites of Logan. Another photo is where he is dressed in his dinosaur Halloween costume. There is also a photo of

Kendra and Logan, and the final one is from our most recent vacation together (roughly a month before he passed away).

We will continue to pray for Lillian's good health. We hope God continues to allow things to go well for you and your family. If you wish to stay in touch, we look forward to hearing from you.

May God Bless you,

Drew, Lisa and Kendra

3/4/18

I cried hysterically on my living room floor. I picked up the pictures that had fallen out of the letter and held them close to my heart. I hugged them so tight, and I cried and cried and cried. I stared at Logan, a beautiful little boy with blonde hair. Chills went down my spine, and my body was covered in goosebumps. How could my heart be so full yet so broken at the same time? My heart ached for this family. I wanted to talk to them and thank them for their selfless act, but I know how long this process can take. I sent my initial letter to this family three months ago. Only God knows how long it will take for me to get in touch with them this time.

I gave considerable thought to what I could do with this information. It took me quite a while to stop crying and staring at this precious boy, Logan, who is now forever living inside Lillian. I sent Jeramy a text that said, "This is Logan, the boy who is the reason why Lillian is still with us. This little boy is forever connected to Lillian through their hearts." He texted back saying he could cry and wanted to know more about Logan and his family as well. I then sent a text to my mom as I prayerfully considered what I could even say to this family. I could feel their pain.

That night, I logged onto Lillian's Facebook page and wrote about how emotional this day had been for me. I wrote about Logan and the circumstances surrounding his death. I discussed how donating an organ is such a selfless act and giving an organ is the best gift anyone could ever bestow on someone. I talked about how emotional it was for me to read Lisa's letter about her son's life and death. Her description of his personality and all of his likes and dislikes, along with the enclosed pictures tore me up inside and made me feel as if I already knew this family. I couldn't wait to talk to them face to face. Within 30 minutes, people were contacting me to say they may know the identity of this family that they had heard their story on the news and thought Logan was the little boy I was talking about. One person sent me his Facebook page, "Love for Logan." I clicked on the link and found myself staring in admiration at a picture of Logan's beautiful face. The page showed videos of Logan, words from his mom, happy memories, and heart-wrenching times. There also were pictures of Logan before the accident and videos of him and his sister playing. These were followed by photos of his hospital stay and of a bruised little boy who now looked blue from losing oxygen. I saw pictures of a mom and dad who had fear, pain, and sadness in their eyes, a pain that I was all too familiar with when Lillian had been on life support. For a moment I just stared at the page, unsure of what to even say—not sure if I should say anything at all. Then I hit the message icon and began typing.

"I am struggling to find the words to say to you … but thank you, thank you, thank you for allowing Logan to be a donor. I can only partially imagine the pain you feel, as Lillian almost died 3 times. One of which, she was on life support for 3 days. Lillian received Logan's aortic valve and other tissue. I opened the mail today and my heart was crushed. Your pictures fell onto my living room floor and I opened the note. I cried hysterically. I am so very sorry for your loss. I just wanted you to know how truly thankful I am. My daughter has a Facebook page … Love for Lillian. I posted about it tonight and turns out we have some mutual people who follow both of our children's journey. I did not share his pictures or the letter, just a little bit of the information. I asked people to pray for you guys. I am praying as well."

Lisa wrote back and asked how I had found her, saying she was grateful that I did. We messaged each other until one in the morning, sharing our stories, our pain and heartbreaks, our lives, similarities, and struggles. We learned that we have several things in common. We each have two children, we both are elementary school teachers, and Lisa was named after Elvis Presley's daughter; my older daughter's name is Preslee. Our Facebook page titles are identical except for the name of each child. They read: "Love for Lillian" and "Love for Logan". We also both chose adorable "L" names for our babies. I was astounded that I was actually talking to the woman whose son had saved my daughter's life. I struggled at times to find the right words to say. I found it difficult to thank Lisa for my child's life when the reason my child was alive was because of her child's death. I get chills just thinking about it. Talking to her filled my heart with both joy and sadness. We logged off of Facebook for the night, agreeing to stay in touch. It was another sleepless night.

In the morning I was still in shock over everything that had happened the night before. It had all happened so quickly. I took Lillian to her nine-month checkup, and the appointment went well. She was still in the negative percentiles for height and weight, but other than that, she looked great. Her brain development also was looking good. I told her pediatrician about us finding the donor family and how grateful we were for them. We sincerely love our daughters' pediatrician. She was my pediatrician when I was little, so I was pleased that she was now treating my daughters. Lillian has become well known at this office, and all of the staff treat us like family. The doctor always takes her time to listen to our concerns and checks Lillian extra closely at each visit. The office staff is wonderful, and we completely trust them with our daughters. I was glad I felt comfortable enough to tell the doctor about the donor family because she understood exactly how I felt about them.

My baby girl had occupational therapy that evening. I gave her therapist a recap of our appointment with the pediatrician, telling her that Lillian still did not appear on the height and weight growth chart curve because she was still in the negative numbers, and that her low weight was still a concern. Her pediatrician is happy with her growth but doesn't want to see her begin to backtrack now that she is starting to hit milestones. She is also burning more calories now that she has greater mobility. At today's therapy session, Lillian is sitting up on her own, and she rolled herself from her back to her belly for the first time. She blows me away with how much she has been through in her short nine months, and she continues to make great strides. She now has a part of Logan inside her. Lillian and Logan share a heart.

The donor bank contacted me to say that they would love to help our family arrange a meeting with the Vanderkleeds. I know this meeting is far more difficult for Lisa than for me because Logan has passed away. I can't even begin to imagine her family's pain. I explained to the donor bank that I was open to meeting the Vanderkleeds when the time was right. Although I had initiated this meeting, I wanted it to take place on God's timing, when Lisa's family felt completely comfortable and ready to meet. Everything surrounding their son's death is still so fresh and new to them, and I wanted to be certain they could cope with the intense emotions that were sure to come with meeting Lillian. I wrote to Lisa and told her that the donor bank had contacted me to say that they would love to arrange for us to meet. I stressed how painful this must be for her and that it wasn't necessary for her to respond immediately. I wanted her to know that if she ever wanted to meet Lillian, I would be more than happy for my daughter to meet the family that had saved her life. After all, Logan's heart is forever a part of Lillian's now.

Lisa and I talk to each other almost every night. Seldom has a day gone by when we have not spoken. We are quickly getting to know each other and are discovering how much we have in common. I placed the letter and pictures she sent to me in a shadow-box I had at home. It made for a tight fit, and I knew I would need a bigger one, but this would have to work until I could get something nicer. I hung it over Lillian's bed so that she will always have Logan looking over her and will forever be reminded of her and Logan's strength.

I bought Lisa's daughter a dress for her birthday to match Preslee and Lillian's dresses. We plan to meet in June, and I am looking forward to spending time with them. Their family will always be a part of my family, and Logan will forever be a part of Lillian. I bought both Lisa and her daughter a necklace, which I plan to give to them when I meet them. I had it customized with Lillian's heartbeat on it—the heartbeat from after her heart repair. In a way, it is both Logan and Lillian's heartbeat because they now share a heart. I also am in the process of having a picture made for the Vanderkleeds that shows our states and has a stethoscope connecting them. It says, "My heart beats because of Logan" and includes the date of Lillian's heart repair surgery, when she received Logan's donor tissue. I know they are not expecting me to bring them a gift. One of the best gifts they will receive is seeing Lillian, the little girl who Logan saved. But I want them to have a reminder of how grateful we are of their decision to donate Logan's organs. Their sacrifice saved our daughter's life, and I could never be more thankful for that act of kindness. God knew that Lillian's heart needed Logan.

The shadow-box in which I originally had placed the note and pictures was too small. I came home one day to find that Lisa had sent me a new and bigger shadow-box in which to display Lillian's heroism. Now we can see all of the pictures, the letter from Lisa and Drew in its entirety, a picture of Lillian, her medical bracelet, and donor card information from the hospital stay in which she received the aorta valve and tissue from Logan. Lastly, I added Lillian's newborn picture in which she is lying on the blanket that says, "God Knew My Heart Needed You." The blanket has several different meanings, but this one finally makes perfect sense.

When I miscarried our second baby, I was devastated. Upon finding out I was pregnant again, I bought the blanket because God knew my heart needed this baby. When Lillian was born, it confirmed how much my heart needed her. After she was placed on life support, I survived by clinging to this blanket. Once again God knew my heart still needed my baby. When we learned that Lillian would receive donor tissue from Logan, I knew God's true purpose in putting the blanket in my hands. Before any of us knew, God knew Lillian's heart needed Logan. The blanket no longer meant that I needed Lillian, even though I truly do need her. God has blessed our family by connecting us to the Vanderkleed family. I was so excited to share this blanket revelation with Lisa that I immediately gathered all of the mementos that were connected to Lillian's heart surgery and took a picture of them in the shadow-box Lisa had given me and sent the picture to her.

In the old shadow-box, I placed the items connected to the time when Lillian was on life support. I placed the painting of her feet made by the child crisis nurse, the doll that was found under the laundry hamper, the one sock that remained on Lillian's foot, a picture of her on life support, and the medical bracelet she had been wearing at the time. I sent both pictures to Lisa and thanked her for her sweet gift of a shadow-box. It was so thoughtful of her to send it, and we will forever cherish it because it came from her and her family. I cannot wait to add more to Lillian's life, room, and memories as we learn more about this loving and caring family and get to meet them.

Chapter 21
The Next Few Months

Life has been pretty good lately. Lillian seems to be in good health and, for the most part, good spirits. She has been teething, so she is a little fussy, but overall she is thriving. She is actually doing better than ever. I've no doubt her warm smile would melt an iceberg. It is so contagious that I can't help but smile every time she does. I find myself becoming more and more nervous as the date of her next cardiology appointment approaches. I thought by now we would not be going to the doctor as often, but Lillian's heart is special, and she will do things her own way.

As the day quickly draws near, I am doing my best to prepare myself for the worst. I still pray continuously that the narrowing of her pulmonary artery will miraculously fix itself, but I know that is not likely to happen. All I want is for Lillian to be given a break for a change. I don't want her to have to be placed under anesthesia again. I just want her to finally get to enjoy being a normal baby. Unfortunately for now, this isn't a likely scenario. But a mother can hope and pray, right?

I am starting to make plans for Lillian's heartiversary, trying to come up with some ideas about what I want to do, but I couldn't think of anything. Jeramy watched the girls on Monday, and when I came home from work, I could not find Lillian's turtle WubbaNub binky anywhere, so I panicked. This binky has been through everything with Lillian. It was there for her heart surgeries, it was there the morning she was placed on life support, and it was what soothed her during her echocardiograms and all of the other tests and procedures. I had to find it. I never realized just how important this silly binky was to me until it went missing. Jeramy claimed he never saw it, but where could it have gone? I began to think about her upcoming echocardiogram and envisioned myself trying to soothe Lillian without having her turtle binky. It would be next to impossible. Fortunately, I found it four days later, and it gave me an idea. I decided to contact WubbaNub and tell them Lillian's story. I included pictures of her with her binky from all the various times she had been in the hospital. I explained to the company how I would love for every heart baby to have a WubbaNub binky to soothe and comfort them throughout their heart journey.

The company contacted me back and offered to sell them to me at wholesale cost. I logged onto the Love for Lillian Facebook page and explained to followers of the page what I wanted to do. I asked if any of Lillian's supporters would like to donate a WubbaNub for the hospital to give to a heart patient, and I received a tremendous response. In just one hour, there were 23 WubbaNubs sponsored. By the next morning, there were already 40 sponsored. I knew there would be even more because some people were sending me checks or paying cash to sponsor a WubbaNub. Two days in, there were over 120 WubbaNubs to donate to hospitalized heart babies. I decided to leave the campaign open until the beginning of May in hopes that the money for the binkies would keep rolling in. We ended the campaign by donating 150 WubbaNub pacifiers to the hospital. I was once again amazed by the generosity of all of Lillian's supporters. They have stuck with us throughout this entire journey and have never failed my family!

Lillian's cardiology appointment went okay. Everyone was happy to see her doing so well at the office. She received a little bear that had an incision just like hers sewn on its chest, which was given to her from another heart family at the office. It was so sweet of them and Lillian loved it. They hooked her up to the pulse-ox machine, and Lillian's oxygen level was at 99 percent. I was so happy to see this number because I was used to it registering much lower. She weighed in at 14 pounds, 14 ounces. She is still pretty small but is slowly gaining weight, so the doctor is happy about that. Everything was going well until the echocardiogram started.

Lillian started to cry instantly. She was not having any of it. I tried everything I could think of to console her. I tried to give her bottle to her, but she pushed it away. I tried to give her snacks to her, but she spit them out. I tried to give her binky to her, but she threw it down. Nothing was working. Lillian did not want anyone to touch her. I even laid on the bed with her and held her. She was perfectly content when no one was touching her, but as soon as someone would, Lillian would start screaming. Unfortunately, when she cries, the echo just looks like a bunch of splatters. We had to find a way to get her to calm down. It took three people, including Dr. G, to try to get her to be still. They eventually were able to get a good enough view to see that Lillian's right pulmonary artery branch is still very narrow. Dr. G said that, other than this, Lillian is doing very well.

He decided that we should go ahead and get a lung perfusion performed on her in June. For this test, they would place an IV and inject a dye into her bloodstream. Then they would look at her lungs to determine how much blood flow is going to each lung. Dr. G believes that Lillian will eventually need a cardiac catheterization to balloon the artery branch and place a stent, but he does not want to have to do that until it is absolutely necessary. The bigger she is, the better. If they were to do it right now, she would not be able to have a stent placed yet because she is still too small. Thankfully, the narrowing is not causing any strain on her heart yet, so waiting is best.

We do not have to have another echo performed until November. The fact that this is six months away terrifies me. But honestly, it is a good thing because it means Lillian is doing well. This will be the longest period of time Lillian has ever gone without an echo or an exam, which makes me nervous.

While at the hospital, we ran into Katie. I was so pleased to see her. She was the one who had been there for me throughout my pregnancy and even held my hand in the delivery room. The last time she had seen Lillian was when Lillian had her first infection. We had been heading to her heart surgeon to have the large white spot on her chest examined because it kept growing and appeared greenish. It had been a scary appointment at that time. It was nice to see Katie and actually have time to talk and for her to see Lillian finally healthy. I took Lillian's picture with Katie because I want my daughter to always remember this compassionate lady who played a huge role in helping me to maintain my sanity after finding out that Lillian had a heart defect.

My sister was giving birth to her baby today— luckily at the same hospital. It was a very good day because Lillian's cardiology appointment went well, I got to see Katie, and now I would get to stay and see my new nephew, who arrived while I was still there. He looks just like my sister. I was happy to see that he was healthy and doing well. I enjoyed getting to cuddle him because I had not cuddled a newborn in a long time. I had missed out on mother-daughter bonding time with Lillian because she was stuck in bed. It was so refreshing to see my nephew being loved on. In this moment, I realized how truly blessed I am to have my baby girls in my life. Even though I did not get to do some of the things that a new mom traditionally gets to do with her newborn, I got to do even better things, including celebrating small milestones that many mothers may take for granted, such as holding my baby, feeding my baby, and changing her diaper.

I feel at peace knowing that Lillian is doing so well. It is crazy to think that we are just on a waiting spree to see how she does. She will need one more open-heart surgery, but Dr. G mentioned that it all depends on her conduit as to when it will take place. He said that the conduit sometimes last six months, five years, or even ten years. For now, we just have to wait it out. Once they are able to place the bigger conduit in her, she hopefully will not require any additional open-heart surgeries. Everything else that needs to be done as she grows older and as the conduit wears should be able to take place in the cardiac cath lab. Lillian will always have a heart condition, but after her next open-heart surgery, everything should be much easier for her. This sets my mind at peace because it is all I have ever wanted for her.

The hospital that performed Lillian's heart surgeries reached out to me on the Love for Lillian Facebook page and asked to feature a story about Lillian on its blog. I was happy to hear this because I love to share her story. It touches my heart to know that Lillian's story can help other people, that her battle has not gone unnoticed. Even though she has seldom gotten a break, she is still here. I am proud to have her as my daughter. Hopefully, Lillian will now inspire other people as she continues to inspire me each day. I am not sure why God chose me to be the mother of the strongest baby in the world, but I sure am happy he did. I have been given the two best daughters in the world.

Lillian had another neurology appointment at which an EEG was performed on her to check for any seizure activity. We then met with her neurologist to discuss where she is at developmentally and possibly getting her off of Keppra. She has a 50 percent chance of having another seizure at some point in her life due to the brain bleeds. There is no way to predict if she will have another episode or not, so in another six months, we plan to see the neurologist again and take her off of Keppra. Hopefully by this time she will be much bigger and will have outgrown her dosage of medicine, so it will be an easy adjustment. From a neurology standpoint, she is about eight months old.

Lillian is currently learning to crawl and has said "dada" and "mom-mom." I am proud of how far she has come. She continuously learns new things and is slowly but surely reaching her milestones. The best one yet, other than saying "mom-mom," is when she gives kisses. When someone asks her for a kiss, she smiles, then opens her droopy mouth real wide, and leans in for the smooch. It is seriously just the cutest thing ever.

I gave a presentation at the hospital for its 101 course at which big donors and other people gather to see how their donations have helped the hospital and its families. I was asked to share parts of Lillian's story with them. They asked me four questions, and I answered them to the best of my ability. I was nervous, but this was important to me. I was way more emotional than I thought I would be. I cried when sharing her story and struggled to get all of the words out.

Question 1: You knew in utero that Lillian had TOF and would be looking at a minimum of two to three corrective surgeries. Your heart surgeon is Dr. H. Describe how you arrived [at this hospital] for Lillian's care and *if* and *how* he and his team and/or resources here have been integral to your faith in choosing [this hospital] and continuing to partner with us for her future care.

My answer: When I went in for my 26-week checkup, I was asked to sit in a comfort room after my ultrasound. After about a ten-minute wait, I started to realize something just didn't seem right. My ob-gyn came in and sat down. She said that the technician noticed something didn't look right. They sent me to the next hospital to see the fetal care team. I felt lost and confused. After an extensive ultrasound, it was determined that our baby has Tetralogy of Fallot. The doctor then sent me to see a pediatric and fetal cardiologist.

He performed a fetal echocardiogram which confirmed the diagnosis. However, it was worse. My baby also had pulmonary atresia. He explained what all it entailed. He handed me a drawing of our baby's heart and wrote four surgeons' names on the paper. He said for us to do our research, but he was pretty sure that with research we would pick the surgeon that he had in mind.

That night my husband and I started our research. We read as much as we could about each surgeon. But we kept coming back to Dr. H. We knew in our hearts that he would be the one to save our baby. When we saw that he worked at this hospital, we were even more thrilled. My husband grew up going here for his cystic fibrosis and I also did for my kidney reflux and thyroid. We knew this was where we were supposed to land. Lillian has been through a lot, but one thing has stayed constant and that is the passion and love everyone here has for their jobs. They have loved Lillian and have always made sure that she was well taken care of. Any questions we have are answered. Any concerns we have are taken seriously. I truly feel that if Lillian would have been anywhere else, we may have lost her. We love this hospital and all of the staff from custodians to surgeons. We will always trust them to care for our daughter.

Question 2: Throughout this roller coaster of a year, you've had several "touch and go" moments, clinically/emotionally/spiritually. You've had decisions to face that no one could ever really prepare you for. How do our staff support you emotionally and spiritually as a parent?

My answer: The staff support us emotionally and spiritually as parents in many ways. First off, they truly take into consideration our fears, questions, and suggestions. This journey has been far from easy. Everybody here seems to remember Lillian and would even stop by her room to check on her when she was not their patient for the day. When Lillian coded for the first time on June 7, 2017, a chaplain was sent to our room. I wanted to kick her out. It's like in all the movies you watch where someone is about to die, so a chaplain comes in and prays for you. I didn't want this to be our reality. I didn't want to say goodbye to Lillian. But the chaplain grabbed my hand and she prayed for Lillian, and the power of prayer was heard when she lived.

A couple months later when I had to start going back to work, I really struggled. Debbie was amazing though and told me I could call or FaceTime her whenever and she would show me Lillian. When Lillian coded again on August 29, 2017, Debbie called me and made sure that I was aware of everything. She offered to call my husband and get me a ride if need be. She wanted me to be there and to make sure I got there safely. She went above and beyond to comfort me.

When I arrived, she greeted me with a hug. The Red Team and Dr. H came out and talked to me and explained all they knew. They were genuine and sincere in explaining what all was going on. They even walked me to her room and gave me space. They always made sure to ask how I was doing and if they could do anything for me. Child life came in on Lillian's three-month birthday and did a painting on a canvas with her footprints. She made three butterflies out of her footprints to resemble each month of her life. This was also the day Lillian had her shunt replaced and successfully came off ECMO. The list goes on and on. They always go above and beyond.

Question 3: Biggest blessing of this hospital?

My answer: The staff. Without all the amazing nurses, doctors, and cardiovascular heart surgeons, Lillian wouldn't still be here. It is as simple as that. They are always alert and catching things quickly. They have all played an important role in Lillian's life and health. Without each and every single one of them and their intelligence, perseverance, love, and passion for what they do, we would have lost Lillian a long time ago. They work well as a team and truly love and care for their patients and families.

Question 4: If you could change or add one thing at this hospital, what would it be?

My answer: The TCU was not the most pleasant place to live in. I know it is in the works to be updated eventually, but it is very outdated and makes things seem gloomier and more depressing honestly. I also wish Beads of Courage were adopted by the hospital. It explains how Debbie and I have already talked about it, but I really wanted this program to be incorporated. It is done for burn patients, cardiac patients, cancer, and a few other areas. It is something that is like a therapy for the parents to do. It's not just for us though. It's such an amazing visual of strength and bravery. Each bead represents something these kids have gone through. One day Lillian will look back at this and actually see what all she has been through. It is her story of strength.

The presentation went very well, and I was happy to be a part of it. Advocating is something I feel I was called to do, and I enjoy telling Lillian's story. I was way more emotional than I thought I would be, and I did cry a couple of times sharing her story, but it felt good to share. There were even a few people in the audience who were crying while I talked about how amazing Lillian is and all she has been through.

June 21 snuck up on us pretty quickly. It was time for Lillian's lung perfusion. She was supposed to have the lung perfusion scan on June 20 at another hospital, but when I received the call to tell me everything they would be doing, I did not feel comfortable with it and chose to cancel. They wanted to fully sedate her, which made me uncomfortable because they said that there would not be anyone from cardiology in attendance or a cardiac anesthesiologist. When they called, they were unaware that Lillian was a cardiac patient and knew nothing of her history. They also thought that she had some sort of feeding tube or gastrostomy button, which she does not. I asked the other moms on a Facebook heart page I follow to explain their experiences with lung perfusions if their heart warrior has had one. Not one of them said their child was sedated, and they also described it as an easy test which normally only takes about fifteen minutes. I knew that I needed further clarification, and I was not going to allow this test to be run on Lillian until I had more answers.

I called the hospital where Lillian's cardiovascular heart surgeon works and asked how they perform lung perfusion scans. The technician explained that it takes about fifteen minutes. They start an IV and then inject a radioactive dye into it. Lillian would then be placed in a machine that can view the dye and take pictures of her lungs as the dye travels through them to determine blood flow to each lung. He said that there was no need to sedate her and that we would quickly be in and out. I liked the sound of this, so I scheduled the test to be performed at Lillian's hospital instead. They were able to get us in the very next day. I am glad I followed my momma instincts because putting Lillian under anesthesia puts her at a high risk and ultimately was not necessary. I can rest easier now, and I feel much better about the lung perfusion scan. I also get to stay in the room with her.

The lung perfusion scan went very smoothly. The technician who runs the test was good with Lillian. He walked us back to the nuclear medicine room and handed Lillian and me a warm blanket. He said the room can sometimes get cold and he wanted us to be comfortable. The child life specialist came to the room as well to help distract Lillian for the IV. We laid her down on the table, and the child life specialist played with toys and played sounds of animals accompanied by pictures on an iPad. This seemed to help Lillian relax. They were able to place the IV on the first stick and get the radioactive medication into her vein to show blood flow to her lungs using the machine. Lillian was not a fan of the IV, but I was impressed when he found a vein on the first stick. She is normally a hard stick, so it was good to have the procedure go so easily.

I was pleased to be able to station myself next to Lillian during the entire scan. Once the prep work was finished, the scan lasted about fifteen minutes. I could see her lungs on the monitor the entire time, which was reassuring. Lillian drank her bottle, randomly cried, and babbled to me the whole time. After the scan, the technician picked up Lillian and talked to her. We then went into the exam room, where he showed me the results of the scan and explained what most of it meant. He said that a doctor still had to review it, but from the appearance of things, it looked pretty good. I was relieved to hear this. I couldn't help but think how easy this had been and how crazy it seemed to me that the other hospital wanted to make a simple procedure much riskier and complicated than it needed to be. I left feeling proud of myself for standing in as Lillian's voice and getting a second opinion.

A couple of days later I received a phone call from Dr. G. The nurse explained that Dr. G looked at the results and it showed that Lillian had 43 percent blood flow in her right lung and 57 percent in her left lung. This means that more blood is going into the left lung than the right due to the narrowing of the right pulmonary artery branch, but it was not significant enough to require an intervention right now. This was the best possible news. This means that Lillian does not need a cardiac cath this summer and that her heart is doing fine, even with the narrowing. Lillian will finally get her big break. We will not need to see Dr. G again until November, which makes me happy but a bit nervous. This will be the longest she has ever gone without seeing her cardiologist, which is fantastic. She will continue to be monitored closely until her heart outgrows the conduit. When that happens, it will be time for her next open-heart surgery. But for now Lillian gets a much-needed break. I cried happy tears for once.

Chapter 22
Meeting the Vanderkleeds

It was finally time to meet the family that gave Lillian the gift of life and thank them in person. The account manager from Senior Donor Services (SDS) reached out to us and paid for our family to stay in a local hotel in Indiana so that we could meet the Vanderkleed family and get to know them better. Lisa and I speak to each other a lot, and I am looking forward to meeting her and her family. They only live four hours away from us, so we decided to drive there. The account manager from SDS is going to meet us there when we arrive.

I am nervous to meet them, and I pray that meeting Lillian will not be too painful for them. Lisa and I have planned a lot of fun activities to do after our initial meeting so that our families can get to know each other. I am not sure what to expect from this meeting, but I trust that God has a plan. Lisa and I have become close over the past couple of months, and I have gained a friendship that will always have a special bond. Our families were brought together by unfortunate circumstances since Logan is not here, but I am thankful God brought us together.

The Indiana Donor Network called me as well. They asked if we would be willing to have our story covered by the local newspaper and media/news station to raise awareness that donations are needed. They said it is very rare for organ tissue donors to actually get to meet the donee because it can be difficult to track who received the tissue. Organ tissue can be stored for up to five years, so the fact that Lillian received donor tissue that was still very fresh, and received it quickly, was very rare. I believed that this would be an opportunity to raise awareness of these donations and agreed to have our story shared through the local media. The Vanderkleeds agreed as well. Lisa actually contacted me before informing the donor bank one way or the other because she wanted my opinion on news coverage first. They are such an amazing family. I knew this would be emotional for them, so I was open to whatever they chose to do. Thankfully, both of our families seem to share the same thoughts and opinions regarding anything having to do with Logan or Lillian.

I packed our bags for the trip the night before we left. I made sure to pack the dress for Kendra, the personalized heartbeat necklaces for Kendra and Lisa, as well as the framed heartbeat picture that we had made for the family. I had a magnet with Logan's picture on it made for Drew to put in his tractor. My first choice was to give Drew a personalized steering wheel knob for his tractor, but I could not find a place that could put Logan's picture on it or engrave it. Instead, I gave him a memory charm to hang on the rearview mirror in his tractor. It has angel wings, a picture of Logan, and a few other memory charms hanging from it. Lisa had informed me that she was pregnant with a baby boy, so I made him a onesie that says, "Hand Picked for Earth by My Brother in Heaven."

We knew the drive would take a little over four hours, so we timed the trip to arrive at 12 pm. We knew the news stations and daily paper would be present and wanted us to be there around 1 pm. We arrived just in time to unload our bags in the hotel and then head to the Vanderkleeds. The drive to Indiana was not too bad, and fortunately for us both Preslee and Lillian slept the majority of the time. We became a little lost because their house was located in the middle of cornfields, but it didn't take us too long to get oriented. When we pulled up to the property, the account manager from SDS and two people from the Indiana Donor Bank met us at our car. They introduced themselves and then explained that a couple of other news stations had shown up. We did not mind because we were excited to be able to spread awareness of organ tissue donation.

Walking around the house to where Lisa, Drew, and Kendra were waiting for us was so nerve-wracking. We had planned to meet at the garden Drew and Lisa had created in memory of Logan. As we turned the corner of their house, we saw a pretty big crowd of people. My first thought was how much taller they were than us. I already knew they were tall, but next to them, Jeramy and I seemed even shorter than we already are. Then reality hit when Lisa had to bend down to hug me.

I was holding Lillian. Lisa hugged me for a long, long time. I knew she was crying, but it wasn't until later when I looked at the pictures that I could see she had been holding Lillian's hand and crying. It broke my heart to see the pictures, but at the same time, it brought me so much happiness. It was exhilarating to actually see them in person. I felt as though I already knew them, considering that Lisa and I have talked almost every day since March, which made it feel more normal.

We talked about the beautiful garden, the drive in from Missouri, and how much both Logan and Lillian drool. The garden was breathtaking. There was a tree planted in honor of Logan, a bench, a small statue, and rocks in the shape of a heart with beautiful messages written on them. Everything was perfect, from the weather to the meeting. We gave the Vanderkleeds their gifts, and they had gifts for us too.

They had shirts made that said, "A living miracle occurred. Two families united through organ/tissue donation." It also had half of a heart that said Logan on it, with a heartbeat leading into a heart-shaped picture of Logan. On the other side was another heartbeat leading to the other half of the heart that said Lillian on it. They also had a canvas made that looked exactly like the shirts. It was absolutely stunning.

Everyone there gave us time to talk a little before asking us questions. Lisa started off talking to one news station, while I talked to another. Jeramy and Drew hung out with Lillian, Preslee, and Kendra The reporter asked me questions about how I felt to meet the donor family, what the tattoo on my arm stood for (which is Preslee's heartbeat leading into half a heart, then the other half of the heart is a CHD ribbon with Lillian's heartbeat after the surgery in which Logan's aortic arch was used), what all Lillian has been through, if she will need more surgeries, and a few other questions.

I was able to stay composed and hold back the tears when answering their questions until they asked me how I would thank the family that gave Lillian life. The tears started to roll down my face as I answered, "I cannot. I can't thank a family and say, *Sorry you lost your son, but my daughter is still here.* But I can say, *Your son is the reason my kid is still alive.*"

I explained to multiple news stations and the daily newspaper that the goal of this meeting was to thank the Vanderkleeds as well as spread awareness for organ and tissue donation. There is no way to truly thank

258

this selfless family, which is the reason why we were there. We hoped this would bring them healing and peace in their decisions during the most difficult time of their lives. My husband said it best when he said to me, "The Vanderkleeds are amazing people. It takes a lot of compassion to know your son is passing away and to spend some of those final moments with him thinking about how your loss could save other people's lives."

After the interviews with all the people there, we went inside the Vanderkleed's home to see Logan's room and get to know each other better. Logan's room was exactly the same as it was when he was alive. It was an adorable elephant-themed room. One of the things that touched me the most was seeing Logan's handprint circled on a mirror to preserve it and keep it from being erased. We all sat around the kitchen table sharing our stories before we went out to eat. We ate at a restaurant that is locally owned, and the food was very good. Drew and Lisa would not let us pay and picked up the tab even though we insisted that we wanted to pay. They truly are thoughtful and generous people.

After dinner, we went back to the Vanderkleed's house and hung out. We watched the news stations air our special story on different channels. We also found internet links to the daily newspaper and read what its reporter had written. It was encouraging to see and read our story because it certainly will spread awareness about organ and tissue donation, which is why we agreed to talk to the media in the first place; plus, it gives both my family and the Vanderkleed's family something else to be happy about. Later that night, Jeramy and I took our girls back to the hotel so we could get some rest.

The next morning, Lisa and Kendra met us at the hotel. We had a fun day of activities planned, things that Logan loved to do. We went to the zoo, which was small but fun. It had a splash pad and a lot of interactive activities for the kids to do. Preslee and Kendra were adorable running around and playing together. Nearby, there was a really cool park with multiple playgrounds for different age levels. Kendra and Preslee had a blast playing on the slides, chasing each other, and climbing on the playground equipment.

When it became too hot and our bellies were hungry, we went back to the car and drove to find a place to eat lunch. We ate pizza and salad, and I quickly paid so Lisa couldn't try to pay again. We ate dessert at a frozen yogurt place that Logan loved. Lisa told us how Logan would always order frozen yogurt and add gummy frogs, his favorite candy, to it. She said he never actually ate the frozen yogurt but instead would pick out every last little piece of candy. Lillian and Preslee also loved the frozen yogurt—it was very tasty. Afterwards, we drove by Logan's gravesite, which had a beautiful headstone with a picture of Logan and tractors on it. Next to his gravestone was a couple of tractor toys, as Logan adored tractors.

We headed back to the Vanderkleed's house so that Preslee and Kendra could swim in their blow-up pool. Lisa also prepared food for dinner. Drew got off work an hour or so after we returned to their house. Preslee and Kendra were having a blast in the pool while we sat around the table outside talking about random things. When the kids were finished swimming, we went inside to eat and watch a couple of movies. Jeramy and I are not very good at card games, so Drew and Lisa taught us a game that we would be able to play with their other family members, who would be coming to their house the next day. It was a little confusing, and it took me longer to catch on than Jeramy, but it was fun. We then ate the delicious chicken that Lisa had prepared, along with potatoes and salad. It was getting late, and we agreed to go to church with the Vamderkleeds in the morning, so we went back to the hotel to sleep.

We woke up early and met Lisa and Drew at their house so that we could follow them to church. We all wore our shirts that Lisa had made for us. When we arrived, we met a lot of their family members and their pastor. Everyone was so nice and welcoming. During the service, the young children were invited to come forward for a children's sermon, and a woman talked to them in front of the congregation in language the kids could understand. Preslee mustered the courage to go up with Kendra, which made me happy. She looked cute sitting there kicking her feet and listening to what the lady was saying, even though she appeared to be a little confused.

Then Preslee and Kendra went back to the Sunday school area, and I checked Lillian into the nursery so that we could listen to the sermon and follow along without any distractions. It was a good service, and afterwards we picked up the kids and everyone socialized while drinking coffee, tea, water, or lemonade. All of the kids went into the gym area and were running around and playing. It was adorable watching Preslee run around with the older kids and try to keep up. Lillian sat there rolling a ball around and scooting around the gym area on her bottom.

After church we went to eat lunch at a wings place with Drew, Lisa, Kendra, and some of Drew's family, including his dad and mom. They were all very sweet people and we had a lot in common. The food was very delicious. Kendra used her quarters to win candy for her and Preslee, which I thought was very sweet. We all talked about our stories, about what all Lillian has gone through, and everything she will have to go through later in life.

When everyone finished lunch, we went back to the cemetery with all of Logan's family to get a picture of Lillian by Logan's gravestone and a picture with both of our families together. We then got back in our cars and went to the Vanderkleed's house, where we played the card game that we had learned the day before. Jeramy and I definitely were not the best players, but we tied for fourth place out of six, so at least we didn't take last place! Lisa prepared a delicious pork dinner with salad, vegetables, and rolls. We spent the rest of the evening talking, playing cards, and getting to know each other better. Kendra and Preslee played downstairs most of the time, and Drew's family spent some time trying to get pictures with Lillian. They all headed home, but we stayed and hung out for a while.

I knew this was our last day together because we had to head back home in the morning. We watched some TV and hung out some more. We had Preslee clean up her messes, and then we had to say our goodbyes. Preslee didn't want to leave, and neither did I. We had a really good weekend, and it made me sad to have to leave. We gave our hugs and agreed to stay in touch. Kendra jumped in our car and was playing with Lillian, saying she didn't want Lillian to go. We said our final goodbyes and then drove back to the hotel. Lisa and I texted that night. At the hotel, I packed our things and got us ready to head home so we could sleep in a little in the morning. We all went to bed.

The next morning, we drove the four hours home. I am thankful we were able to meet the Vanderkleeds. They are some of the sweetest people I have ever met and will forever be a huge part of our lives. I pray we stay in touch and that we can get together again sometime soon. I can't wait to see the sweet pictures of their new baby boy when he is born and to continue to get to know this amazing family. Lillian will always know about Logan—the little boy who saved her life!

Chapter 23
A Year in Review

As I sit back and reflect on this past year, I can't help but see everything as a blur. I am so grateful that I recorded every single heartbreaking and heartwarming event: I kept a journal, I asked the tough questions, and I was there for Lillian throughout this crazy year. My sweet baby girl has been through so much. She was born a blue baby and wasn't able to eat milk until she was a week and a half old. She has endured more in her life than any baby (or adult for that matter) should ever have to go through, and she has survived three heart surgeries.

Lillian has had surgery for an infection growing toward her heart. She has lived in the hospital for sixty-four days (not including all of the days she had doctor appointments outside of the hospital). She has survived three days on life support, has had three cardiac arrests, and has had compressions done on her freshly cut-open chest on three different occasions. She has had seven seizures for which the doctors and nurses had to intervene to get her breathing again. She has many scars covering her chest, side, neck, and wrist. I have seen her heart rate skyrocket well over 200 and into the 220s. I have watched her heart rate drop into the 60s and then bounce back into the 100s. Her oxygen levels have been as low as 19, and her heartbeat has dropped into the 20s when she went into cardiac arrest.

Her heart condition has caused me so much stress and worry in this life, but she is my daily reminder to be thankful and never take anything for granted. She has taught me so much. She is beautiful, and she is a child of God. She is my smiles in the morning and the reason I found my faith in God. She is nothing less than perfect. Her scars show the most beautiful and breathtaking story of survival. And although I have spent many days this year terrified of the what if's and the trials, I am smiling. I am a better person because of Lillian.

We celebrated our warrior's first birthday and her sister's third birthday on June 2. We chose a date in between both of their birthdays for the party because Lillian's birthday is May 31 and Preslee's is June 12. We celebrated a life that Lillian was not promised, a milestone that I was terrified we would not reach at times. It seems as though this year has flown by. We celebrated the joyous occasion with all of our close friends and family.

Not only did we celebrate a first birthday, but we celebrated a beautiful girl who was born into this world having to face bigger battles than anyone could imagine, and yet she is still here. We honored a girl who has a purpose in this life, a girl who still smiles when she has every reason in the world to be angry.

The birthday party theme was "*Donut* grow up!" Lillian is now age one and Preslee turns three in ten days. Watching their love for one another takes my breath away. Even though I don't want my babies to grow up so quickly, it sure does beat the alternative. I am proud to watch my girls grow up together. I feel like the most blessed mom in the world. I get to watch two beautiful girls grow up; it doesn't get any better than that.

It is so crazy to think that if Lillian would have been born in the mid-1940s, she would not be here. Seventy-eight years ago there was no known way to repair her heart. The BT shunt had not been created yet, and she would have died shortly after birth from the inability to breathe. As far as ECMO goes, it wasn't successfully created/used until 1975, so if she had been born before then, she would have passed away on her birthdate. I thank God every day for medical technology and advancements and for the knowledge acquired by amazing cardiovascular heart surgeons, cardiologists, doctors, and nurses.

In addition to this adult book, I am in the process of publishing two children's books. I wanted Lillian to have a good book that she can read as she gets a little older that shows her and other people the bravery and strength of heart warriors. I wanted my words to bring comfort to other heart warriors as well. I titled the book, "A Heart Warrior's Beauty Marks" because Lillian is a true warrior, and I refer to her scars as her "beauty marks."

After writing this book, I couldn't help but think about how the siblings of heart warriors sometimes feel left out, so I was inspired to write my second children's book, titled, "Sibling of a Heart Warrior." I dedicated this book to Preslee, who has been through so much during the past year. She went from being an only child to having to share her mommy and daddy. On top of that, she had to spend a lot of time away from us while we took care of Lillian in the hospital. She was a trooper through it all. I feel heart warrior siblings are warriors in their own right and deserve recognition.

As far as our personal lives go, Jeramy and I are learning to communicate better. We lost our way at times during the past year, but we are slowly getting back to being ourselves. We have been fighting tough battles since we were fifteen and seventeen. We have grown up together and have gone through many trials that would tear many couples apart. We have dealt with silly highschool drama and debilitating cystic fibrosis. We have been challenged by learning how to be married and live together and by heartbreaking fertility issues. None of these things even come close in comparison to everything we have battled over the past year.

We found out that we had miscarried, and then shortly thereafter discovered we were pregnant again and were about to be heart parents. We have lived through heart surgeries, unplanned hospital stays, being apart for days to weeks at a time, and nearly losing our daughter multiple times. I know there are many more battles we will have to fight in the future. We have learned to be thankful for what we have been given. We are happy to be able to look back at everything we have been through and realize we have survived it. Our family is still together, as we should be. We have survived the most stressful situations ever, and we are going to stick it out not only for our babies, but also for each other. We cope with things differently and don't always see eye to eye, but we have vowed to stay together in sickness and in health, in good times and bad, until death do us part, and we meant every single word. Being together is better than being apart, and our relationship takes work like any other, but we love each other and will do whatever it takes to make our marriage work.

Not only were we working on our relationship with each other, but we decided to work on our relationship with God and began attending church with the girls. I had promised God that I would better myself and would honor him if he would let Lillian live. I didn't really know how to pray, and I was still wrestling with my faith. When I look back on that prayer now, I realize it was the desperate plea of a mother whose child was on the verge of death. I hope that even if Lillian had earned her angel wings, I would have still found a way to love and honor God and his plan for my life. The more I attend church, the more I realize that I have no control over my own life. The only things I have control of now are my decisions, my faith, and how I choose to live my life. I was saved when I almost lost Lillian. Now I understand how to pray with sincerity and faith, how to be a better Christian, and most importantly, how to honor God no matter what his plan is for me, my marriage, and both of my children.

I have thoroughly enjoyed the church services. I am learning so much, and attending church truly has helped me to develop a positive view of things. I did not grow up in a church, so I have a lot more to learn about being a citizen in the kingdom of God, but I am happy that Jeramy, the girls, and I are going to church together as a family. We take Preslee to the church's preschool program and she loves it. I will never force her to attend church because I believe that I have a stronger connection with God now that I have chosen to accept his invitation to visit him at his house each week instead of being forced to go. I want Preslee and Lillian to learn about Jesus though. I did not know much about him growing up, and I don't want them to feel lost in their faith, as I have during the past year.

I have now seen the power of prayer at work in

my family. I am thankful to God for walking alongside, and sometimes even carrying, my family and Lillian throughout this journey. He has continued to love me even when I have questioned him. I am learning now that Lillian's illness is not his fault. He is not the reason she has a CHD, he is not the reason Lillian has repeatedly broken the rules, and he is not the reason we have almost lost her so many times. Rather, he is the reason why Lillian is still here, the reason why I still get to be her mommy, and the reason why there are amazing cardiologists, nurses, and cardiovascular heart surgeons to take care of Lillian.

I try my best to reach out to other mothers of heart warriors. I feel as though it is my calling to support other heart moms now and to tell Lillian's story to inspire others. Every parent recalls her "worst" moment with her child, although "worst" varies by experience, and everyone has different experiences. Before Lillian was born, Preslee was hospitalized for kidney issues and a virus. She has stage three reflux, which means that her urine backtracks into her kidneys. This causes infections and will most likely result in the need for her to have surgery at the end of the year. Only time will tell. That was my worst moment as a parent at the time. Little did I know that my worst was about to be a billion times worse when Lillian arrived.

Any time a child goes through some sort of trial, a good parent will think it is the worst that could happen.

I am very blessed in this regard because, although Lillian's condition is way worse than most people can imagine, hers is not the worst case in the world. I am able to acknowledge that and therefore am grateful that her story is not the worst.

I would not trade my new normal for anything because I am thankful that Lillian is still here. I want other heart moms to feel they are not alone. When time and money allow, I enjoy donating to the NICU and PICU that saved Lillian's life. It brings me great joy to shine light on such a heart-wrenching diagnosis to other parents. Each year on her heartiversary, which we will celebrate on December 27 this year because it is the day her heart was "repaired," I will bring some sort of snack, personalized cookies, or other things to the hospital to give to the amazing staff who saved Lillian's life and helped to comfort me and keep me sane through this rocky journey.

However, the journey is far from over. Lillian's conduit will need to be replaced as her heart grows. She will require more heart surgeries and will need the conduit replaced as it wears out. Lillian has never followed the rules, and I'm sure that will stand true for the rest of her life. Each patient is different. Some require pacemakers, while others have no problems at all. Some patients' conduits shrink, and they require intervention sooner, while others don't. There is no way

to tell what Lillian's future holds. As her mommy all I can do is love her and give her what she needs.
Lillian has always been a rule breaker, but I needed to find a way to trust her. I have to trust that God will protect her when I cannot. She has been recovering well and has started to smile again and even laugh. She is slowly reaching milestones, such as crawling, even though she looks like a monkey because of the way she moves her legs; it is the weirdest but cutest crawl I have ever seen. She is waving and bringing food to her mouth. She loves to say "da-da" and "mom-mom." She makes loud popping noises with her mouth and moves her tongue back and forth quickly. She is such a happy baby.

We still struggle to get her to eat enough, and she is still in the negative percentiles for weight and height. She is making gains each day though, and a nutritionist is starting to work with us to help her gain weight. She continues to learn new things. We have no way of telling if her brain bleeds will cause damage in the future. Neurology is hopeful that they will not cause any delays, but only time will tell.

Lillian's Beads of Courage strand continues to grow and will continue to do so throughout her life. I will keep adding to her strand as appointments, surgeries, procedures, and other events come up. I don't know what life has in store for Lillian, but I believe she will do something big. She is so strong, and her story is far from over. The beads are a good visual of all she has overcome and all she will become. The beads are my therapy for now, but I know they will be her therapy when she is older. I pray that she will be as proud of herself as I am of her. Her strength and bravery at such a young age is indescribable. Her beads are the light in her dark journey. Sometimes everything seems so black and white. This journey is very scary and there is still so much unknown. But these beads represent all Lillian has overcome. They bring bright color to this darkness; Lillian herself is my light in the darkness. One day I know she will love to look at her bead necklaces and see what kept me going and see how truly amazing she is.

I started to volunteer in the hospital as well. I love to share Lillian's story, and I want to be there for other families of heart babies. In the beginning I felt so alone. I want other families to know that they are never alone on this journey. I pray that Lillian's story will inspire others as she inspires me.

I volunteered to help out with events hosted by the hospital in relation to family support, public speaking, and whatever else they need me to do. I will also be giving a presentation to medical assistants and other people in the medical field in October. My mom asked me if I would be willing to share Lillian's story at the Missouri Medical Chapter's annual meeting, at which she presides as president, so that we could spread awareness of CHD and organ/tissue donation. It just so happens that this event takes place in the same hospital at which Lillian's cardiologist works and where Lillian was born. I know that God chose me to be Lillian's mom for a reason. Although I do not always know the reasons for everything, I know that it is now my calling to be an advocate for heart warriors. I won't stop! I thoroughly enjoy spreading awareness and giving back when possible. This, too, is my therapy in a way.

I'm learning to cope. Although I still struggle deeply with depression and PTSD, I don't talk about it. Even if you know me and see me every day, you probably wouldn't notice. I am good at hiding it. Most days are better than others. There are still days in which I feel useless in this life, and I struggle to find myself, but I'm trying. I do it for my kids. I'm exhausted, but I love my babies more than life itself, so I keep moving forward for them. They are my reason to keep pushing on. They are the light in my dark world and are the reason why I wake up each morning and try to better myself.

Maybe one day I'll seek counseling and try to cope with the images that have permanently scarred my brain. Perhaps one day I'll find a way to forgive myself for failing my daughters. But until then I'll keep smiling. I'll keep doing what I do for my babies and continue to push forward and be their voice.

Dates ring in my head constantly. Lillian has been through so much this past year, and it saddens me. Many people do not understand why I struggle on certain dates. They just don't get why many dates are permanently etched in my memory. I am thankful they haven't had to feel the heartache that those dates have brought to me. It isn't necessarily the dates that trigger me, but it is the memories and the things I have seen on those days. Each year on those particular dates, horrible images will race through my mind. It is difficult to have those images indelibly stored in my brain, but in the end, Lillian is still here with me, and I try my best to focus on that. Sometimes though, my PTSD gets the best of me.

Lillian has developed a fear that is heartbreaking: She doesn't trust anyone. If someone she doesn't know walks into the room, she instantly clings to me. She tries to climb over my shoulders to get as far away as possible from the stranger. She screams and cries and doesn't stop until the person leaves the room. Some people look at her behavior and think she's just spoiled or just acting rotten. But inside, it breaks me. I know she is doing it because it reminds her of what has happened. It's not just a stranger-danger thing; it's a legitimate scared-out-of-her-mind fear. I dread going to doctor appointments with her or to her next echocardiogram. I hate seeing my sweet baby girl scared beyond belief. No baby should have to experience this kind of fear and anxiety or know pain to this extent. All I can do is be there for her and pray for her.

In the end, all of this is what it is. I have learned to accept the things I cannot change and to change the

276

things I can. I will protect Lillian the same way I protect Preslee. I don't want to limit her or make her feel different. I have to learn to let her live and to face my own fears or I will only hold her back. I am her mommy, and it is my job to teach her to love herself and to be proud of her scars/beauty marks. Lillian has taught me so much more about life than I have ever known. I owe God, all of the doctors, Dr. H, Dr. G, and her nurses my life. They are the reason Lillian is still here.

I also owe mine and Jeramy's families everything. They have taken on the role of caring for Preslee when we couldn't. They have experienced every heartache with us. They have cried with us, brought us food, and given us their full support every step of the way. I have learned to find strength when I thought there was none. I have also learned to just roll with the punches. I still have my bad days. I am a worrier at heart and always prepare for the worst. I am learning that although being a heart mom is hard, it is the most rewarding title I have earned. I am living in a world that I didn't ask to be in and would never wish on anyone else, but I wouldn't change it for the world.

I will always be by Lillian's side, advocating for her. I will never give up on her. I will fight with every breath in my body, just as she does. I will dedicate my life to watching Lillian fight for her life, whether in the hospital or at home. I now live a life in which I know more about the heart and medical field than I ever could have imagined.

I will forever be paranoid about Lillian's health, and I am terrified for the moment to come when I am told it is time for Lillian's next open-heart surgery. I know it will be here before I know it, but I have placed it in God's hands, along with everything else in my life. God is in control! Whatever his plan may be, I am thankful for the time I've had with my daughter, and I will cherish every day I have with her. I am now in a world with amazing heart moms who are just like me. New problems will most likely arise with Lillian, but I know she will fight with all she has in her. Lillian is my hero! I cannot thank all of her supporters enough for their continued prayers and their unwavering Love for Lillian.

He heals the brokenhearted and binds up their wounds.
(Psalm 147:3, NIV)

*The Lord will fight for you, and you have only to be
silent.* (Exodus 14:14, ESV)

*Is anyone among you sick? Let him call for the elders of
the church, and let them pray over him, anointing him
with oil in the name of the Lord. And the prayer of faith
will save the one who is sick, and the Lord will raise him
up.* (James 5:14-15, NKJV)

*"For I know the plans I have for you," declares the
Lord, "plans to prosper you and not to harm you, plans
to give you hope and a future."* (Jeremiah 29:11, NIV)

A poem for Lillian (written before we received the news that her pulmonary artery was already narrowing).

The Life of Lillian

Lillian, my sweet baby girl,
you inspire me in every way.
I look at you and smile, my dear,
for you've survived another day.
I could not wait to welcome you
that special day when you arrived,
but fear of the unknown struck me,
as I laid in my bed and cried.

I badly wanted to meet you.
Are we having a boy or girl?
But the moments of my pushing,
threw everyone into a whirl.
Your heart rate then dropped way too low.
"Stop pushing," all the doctors said.
As fear then swallowed up the room,

I lay helpless and filled with dread.

"We have to pull your baby out;
side effects are common with this.
We are out of other options;
the heart rate is sadly amiss."
"It's a girl!" your daddy then said.
I could hardly believe my eyes.
You were so beautiful but blue,
so we needed to hear your cries.

Then silence filled the tiny room;
and I heard music to my ears.
The sound of your soft, gentle cries
filled my eyes with some joyful tears.

I wanted to hold you close, love,
to keep you warm in my embrace.
You went to the NICU
while I tried to recall your face.

The first echocardiogram
confirmed what the heart doctor said,
that Tetralogy of Fallot
is the reason you're stuck in bed.
Since you cannot breathe on your own,
the medicines keep you alive.
With open-heart surgery soon,
you'll have a great chance to survive.

Three long hours went steadily by
before I was wheeled to your room.
Seeing all the lines and the wires
gave me more than a sense of doom.

I wish I could somehow mend you.
No, this is not the least bit fair.
Now I have become a heart mom,
and it is my burden to bare.

I have doubted myself today.
I could not give you what you need

so I turned to God our Father,
"Let me take her place," I would plead.
Just knowing I could not hold you,
that I could never take your place,
I sat in that hospital room
wiping tears that streamed down my face.

My mind became filled with darkness,
and anger consumed every thought.
How could this happen to you, dear?
I only became more distraught.

I did not feel like a new mom;
excitement was stolen from me.
I could not hold you or feed you
or even change you when you peed.

Surgery day did soon arrive;
there was just no way to prepare.
"Make sure my baby stays alive!"
to God I sincerely declared.

It was much too hard to focus.
My phone was still glued to my side.
waiting for the call to tell me
that you, my sweet baby, survived.

I thank God the phone finally rang.
"She did well," her heart surgeon said.
"We are closing her up right now,
but you will soon be by her bed."

At last, I finally saw you;
I could hardly believe my eyes.
You did not look like my baby.
I tried hard to hold in my cries.

I hate that you must go through this,
with your chest cut open and more;
there's a tube placed down your throat now,
IVs, and drainage lines galore.
They tried to take you off the vent,
but you simply needed more time.

You were too tired, thank goodness,
because your health quickly declined.

Your heart rate dropped way down too low.
You stopped breathing all on your own.
The doctors quickly came running;
no longer were we left alone.

I begged God to please let you live;
I wasn't ready to say goodbye.
You coded twice on that morning.
To Satan, I shouted, "Good try."

With some time you healed quite nicely;
steps forward with progress were made.
Within two weeks we brought you home.
I'm so thankful you're strong and brave!
But your oxygen levels dropped,
and two big puss pockets appear.
You had to have a CT scan,
which confirmed the heart surgeon's fear.

Your incision is infected,
and it's now growing toward your heart.
You need another surgery;
Tomorrow morning they will start.

Thank goodness we caught it early;
this could have turned bad really fast.
You will stay in the PICU
as long as bacteria lasts.

Recovery wasn't easy;
a big problem started to grow.
Your little heart quickly gave out;
you were placed on ECMO.
Your heart needs time to recover;
they'll give it a day, maybe two.
They are not sure why this happened;
they're figuring out what to do.

I locked myself in the bathroom

and cried, curled up on the floor.

I went to your PICU room

and heartbroken, looked through your door.

Another unfair obstacle

that you, baby, now have to face.

I had to leave it up to God

and pray for his mercy and grace.

They think they have found the problem,

and are hoping that it will work.

Another open-heart surgery,

the silence could drive me beserk.

Because hope is never certain,

and they did not have a plan B,

they knew they had to try something,

a new BT shunt it would be.

The purple team rushed in quickly,

and I saw them wheel you away.

"I love you. Please be strong for me,"

is all I could muster to say.

We got the call that you did well,
now breathing, heart beating again.
You came off of ECMO;
now recovery can begin.

You suffered through seven seizures
that the EEG could not trace.
I watched each time you stopped breathing;
you had a blank stare on your face.
They started you on medicine,
and then no more seizures occurred.
Another obstacle conquered,
but your heart problem still wasn't cured.

Thirty days in the hospital
was more than a long enough stay.
I was happy when I brought you home;
I had prayed so hard for this day.

When only four short months later
it was time for your heart repair,
another open-heart surgery;
we did not have enough time to prepare.

Still terrified of the what ifs
and all that could maybe go wrong,
I tried to stay strong and patient;
I know this procedure is long.
Now I am nervously waiting;
it seems like we never have left.
Ended up in the same room again,
and that threw me into distress.

Of course, this would be the same room
in which I had said my goodbyes.
The room where we nearly lost you,
the room in which you almost died.

I was terrified to be there;
bad memories flooded my mind.

I tried so hard to bury them,
but bad thoughts always stay confined.

You made it out of surgery,
and your VSD is now closed.
No complications to report,
as your conduit helped blood flow.
Recovery was so easy,
as nothing seemed out of the norm.
They kept a watchful eye on you;
you've hated rules since you were born.

Your incisions are healing nicely.
You went home on day number nine.
Everything is going so well,
and you are adjusting just fine.

You'll finally get a nice break,
one that you, baby, have earned.
No surgeries for a long time.
I think of the things you will learn.

No surgeries scheduled for now,

so you can continue to grow.

You'll still do it Lillian's way;

We'll simply just go with the Fallot (flow).

I still wish that I could mend you,

as none of this seems at all fair.

But now I am a proud heart mom,

and your story I'll proudly share.

Love, Mommy

An Open Letter to Dr. H

Dear Dr. H,

I have tried to thank you in many ways for all you have done for Lillian, but whatever I do or say will never be enough. You have given Lillian the life that she and all babies deserve. Without you, she would not be here today.

When we discovered that Lillian had a CHD, I felt like my world was ending. Nothing made sense to me, and I feared the worst. We were told that we needed to choose a heart surgeon and were given a list of four names. I remember thinking, is that all? Only four choices? But that ended up being more than we needed. With extensive research, we quickly made our decision and have never looked back or second guessed ourselves. We felt completely confident in choosing you.

We didn't know how truly blessed we were to have selected you at first. It was so terribly hard to trust someone we didn't know to work on our baby's heart and bring her back to us alive. Sitting in a hospital waiting room, praying for not only my baby, but for the surgeon and surgical team that would be operating on her as well, has proven to be extremely difficult.

Your dedication to saving lives is miraculous. I hope you never doubt how truly amazing you are. Living in the hospital with Lillian, I saw more than most parents do. I saw nurses endlessly working, doctors tirelessly staring at a wall of monitors, custodians graciously mopping floors, heartbroken people crying, and so much more. But you, Dr. H, never went unnoticed.

I watched you during your rounds each day, roughly around 6 to 7 am and 5 to 6 pm. The times varied depending on what procedures were scheduled for surgery and what was happening on the PICU and TCU floors. I watched you drink your coffee while you fully listened to nurses and families during rounds.

I think of all the times you entered Lillian's room and listened ever so closely to her heart and stared at her machines that were beeping. You would talk to Lillian and try to determine what was going on with her when things weren't going as planned (even though she couldn't talk or answer you). I remember your blank stare, just looking at her as you rubbed your chin with your hand, determined to find answers. Everything you did for our daughter never went unnoticed.

You sacrifice so much of your time and your life for heart babies, and I pray for you every single day. It takes a truly selfless man to dedicate his life to saving other people's lives, yet that is exactly what you do. You are remarkable and deserve the world and more.

When I think about Lillian's future now, I think of you. She would have no future without you. You have saved her life countless times. Everyone in this world deserves a person in their life like you. I hung a picture in Lillian's bedroom of you holding her, so she will always see the face of the man who never gave up on her, the man who found the answers that saved her life.

Lillian has more surgeries to come, and I pray that God will continue to guide your hands and help you to save her life when it is time for her next heart surgery. I am absolutely terrified for that day to arrive, but I believe in you, which brings comfort to my soul. I could not imagine having to choose someone to operate on Lillian's heart again if you were not on the list of choices. I don't think we would be able to find a mind as brilliant or hands as skilled as yours. I would not be able to trust another cardiac surgeon as I do you, because you are the best.

You are forever a fundamental piece to our lives. Our puzzle would not be complete without you. I can't even begin to imagine the amount of lives you have saved, the number of families that are forever changed for the better because of you. Maybe you aren't even aware of how truly amazing you are and how thankful my family is to know you. That's one reason why I wanted to write you this letter. I'm sure thousands of other families feel the same way about you as I do.

When Lillian went on life support, I thought my life was ending. I didn't want to live in a world without her. I was in a very dark place. But you didn't give up on her. You saved her life by placing her on ECMO, and then you saved her life again by operating on her and getting her off ECMO. Little did you know that you saved two lives that day, because I was slowly able to crawl out of that dark place, knowing Lillian's time wasn't over yet.

We love you, Dr. H, and we will always talk about you and cherish you in our home. You will never be forgotten. Your hard work and dedication will never go unnoticed. I pray that when the time comes for you to retire, your family gets to spend every waking moment with you. I pray you will get to make up for all the lost time with your family, who I'm sure missed your presence all those times you were busy saving lives, and that you never have a worry in the world. I pray you never doubt the impact you have made on thousands of families and accept credit for all the lives you have saved. I pray you have the best life ever!

Although you wear a lab coat and stethoscope instead of a costume and cape, you are a true superhero in our eyes. Our vision of superheroes has changed dramatically since Lillian was born! Thank you again, Dr. H, even though Thank You will never be enough!

Love, The Wilsons

May 31, 2017- Lillian was born

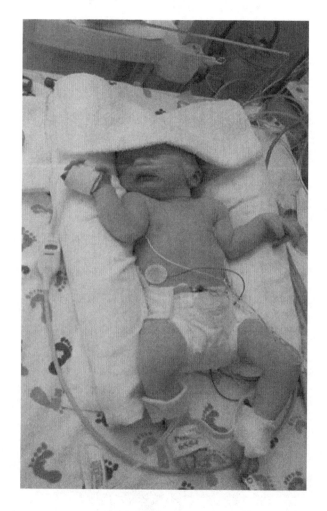

June 5, 2017- BT Shunt Placed

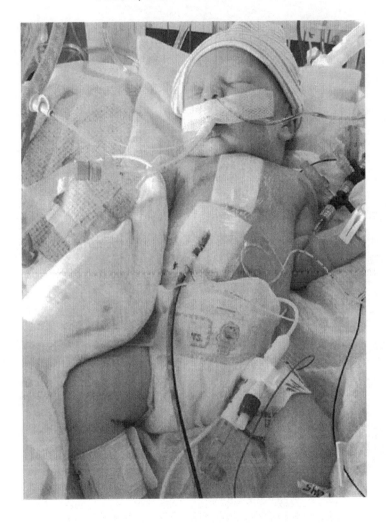

August 16, 2017- Wound Vac

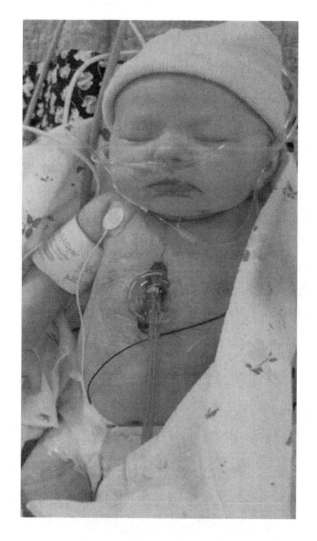

August 29, 2017- Lillian hooked to ECMO

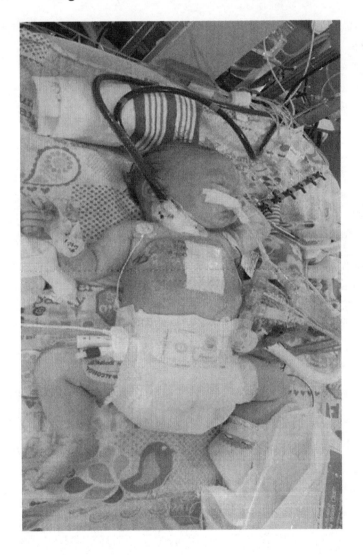

August 30, 2017: Possible Seizures

August 31, 2017- New BT Shunt and off ECMO

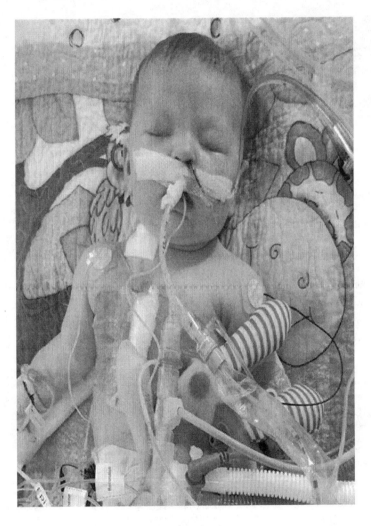

September 5, 2017- EEG for 7 seizures

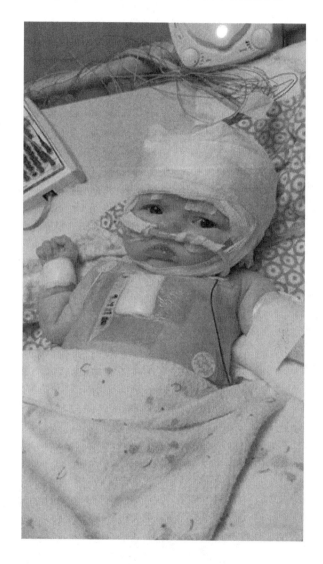

September 25, 2017- Bloody Stools

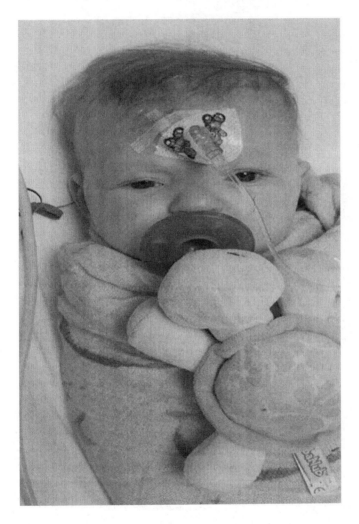

December 27, 2017- TOF with PA repair

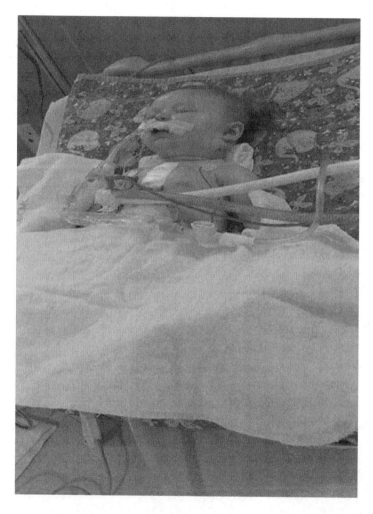

Lillian with her Beads of Courage

Meeting the Vanderkleeds

The Wilsons and the Vanderkleeds by Logan's grave

Lillian by Logan's Grave!